Hebrews

Hebrews

Daniel J. Harrington
with Little Rock Scripture Study staff

LITURGICAL PRESS
Collegeville, Minnesota

littlerockscripture.org

Nihil obstat for the commentary text by Daniel J. Harrington: Robert C. Harren, *Censor deputatus.*
Imprimatur for the commentary text by Daniel J. Harrington: ✠ John F. Kinney, Bishop of St. Cloud, Minnesota, December 29, 2005.

Cover design by John Vineyard. Interior art by Ned Bustard. Photos and illustrations on pages 32, 42, and 55 courtesy of Getty Images and page 67 courtesy of Wikimedia Commons. Diagram on page 55 courtesy of the *Little Rock Catholic Study Bible.*

This symbol indicates material that was created by Little Rock Scripture Study to supplement the biblical text and commentary. Some of these inserts first appeared in the *Little Rock Catholic Study Bible*; others were created specifically for this book by Michael DiMassa.

Library of Congress Cataloging-in-Publication Data

Names: Harrington, Daniel J. author | Little Rock Scripture Study Staff author
Title: Hebrews / Daniel J. Harrington with Little Rock Scripture Study staff.
Description: Collegeville, Minnesota : Liturgical Press, [2025] | Series: Little Rock Scripture Study | Summary: "This New Testament text presents Jesus as the great High Priest who simultaneously offers sacrifice to God and is himself the sacrifice. His compassion is rooted in his humanity, for he is like us in all things but sin. Harrington's accessible commentary helps us read and reflect on this Scripture text, giving us a renewed appreciation for the saving work of Jesus. Commentary, study and reflection questions, prayers, and access to online lectures are included. 6 lessons"— Provided by publisher.
Identifiers: LCCN 2025020111 (print) | LCCN 2025020112 (ebook) | ISBN 9798400802249 trade paperback | ISBN 9798400802263 epub
Subjects: LCSH: Jesus Christ—Priesthood | Bible. Hebrews—Textbooks | Bible. Hebrews—Biblical teaching
Classification: LCC BS2775.55 .H37 2025 (print) | LCC BS2775.55 (ebook)
LC record available at https://lccn.loc.gov/2025020111
LC ebook record available at https://lccn.loc.gov/2025020112

TABLE OF CONTENTS

Welcome	7
What materials will you use?	8
How will you use these materials?	8
Lesson One (Introduction and Hebrews 1–2)	11
Lesson Two (Hebrews 3:1–5:10)	27
Lesson Three (Hebrews 5:11–7:28)	39
Lesson Four (Hebrews 8:1–10:18)	51
Lesson Five (Hebrews 10:19–11:40)	65
Lesson Six (Hebrews 12–13)	77
Praying with Your Group	89
Reflecting on Scripture	91

Wrap-Up Lectures and Discussion Tips for Facilitators are available for each lesson at no charge. Find them online at LittleRockScripture.org/Lectures/Hebrews.

Welcome

The Bible is at the heart of what it means to be a Christian. It is the Spirit-inspired word of God for us. It reveals to us the God who created, redeemed, and guides us still. It speaks to us personally and as a church. It forms the basis of our public liturgical life and our private prayer lives. It urges us to live worthily and justly, to love tenderly and wholeheartedly, and to be a part of building God's kingdom here on earth.

Though it was written a long time ago, in the context of a very different culture, the Bible is no relic of the past. Catholic biblical scholarship is among the best in the world, and in our time and place, we have unprecedented access to it. By making use of solid scholarship, we can discover much about the ancient culture and religious practices that shaped those who wrote the various books of the Bible. With these insights, and by praying with the words of Scripture, we allow the words and images to shape us as disciples. By sharing our journey of faithful listening to God's word with others, we have the opportunity to be stretched in our understanding and to form communities of love and learning. Ultimately, studying and praying with God's word deepens our relationship with Christ.

Hebrews

The resource you hold in your hands is divided into six lessons. Each lesson involves personal prayer and study using this book and the experience of group prayer, discussion, and wrap-up lecture.

If you are using this resource in the context of a small group, we suggest that you meet six times, discussing one lesson per meeting. Allow about 90 minutes for the small group gathering. Small groups function best with eight to twelve people to ensure good group dynamics and to allow all to participate as they wish.

Some groups choose to have an initial gathering before their regular sessions begin. This allows an opportunity to meet one another, pass out books, and, if desired, view the optional intro lecture for this study available on the "Resources" page of the Little Rock Scripture Study website (littlerockscripture.org).

Every Bible study group is a little bit different. Some of our groups like to break each lesson up into two weeks of study so they are reading less each week and have more time to discuss the questions together at their weekly gatherings. If your group wishes to do this, simply agree how much of each lesson will be read each week, and only answer the questions that correspond to the material you read. Wrap-up lectures can then be viewed at the end of every other meeting rather than at the end of every meeting. Of course, this will mean that your study will last longer, and your group will meet more times.

WHAT MATERIALS WILL YOU USE?

The materials in this book include:

- The text of Hebrews, using the New American Bible, Revised Edition as the translation.
- Commentary by Daniel J. Harrington (which has also been published separately as part of the New Collegeville Bible Commentary series).
- Occasional inserts highlighting elements of the chapters of Hebrews being studied. Some of these appear also in the *Little Rock Catholic Study Bible* while others are supplied by staff writers.
- Questions for study, reflection, and discussion at the end of each lesson.
- Opening and closing prayers for each lesson, as well as other prayer forms available in the closing pages of the book.

In addition, there are wrap-up lectures available for each lesson. Your group may choose to purchase a DVD containing these lectures or make use of the video lectures available online at no charge. The link to these free lectures is: LittleRockScripture.org/Lectures/Hebrews. Of course, if your group has access to qualified speakers, you may choose to have live presentations.

Each person will need a current translation of the Bible. We recommend the *Little Rock Catholic Study Bible*, which makes use of the New American Bible, Revised Edition. Other translations, such as the New Jerusalem Bible or the New Revised Standard Version: Catholic Edition, would also work well.

HOW WILL YOU USE THESE MATERIALS?

Prepare in advance

Using Lesson One as an example:

- Begin with a simple prayer like the one found on page 11.

- Read the assigned material for Lesson One (pages 12–21) so that you are prepared for the weekly small group session.
- Answer the questions, Exploring Lesson One, found at the end of the assigned reading, pages 22–25.
- Use the Closing Prayer on page 25 when you complete your study. This prayer may be used again when you meet with the group.

Meet with your small group

- After introductions and greetings, allow time for prayer (about 5 minutes) as you begin the group session. You may use the prayer on page 11 (also used by individuals in their preparation) or use a prayer of your choosing.
- Spend about 45–50 minutes discussing the responses to the questions that were prepared in advance. You may also develop your discussion further by responding to questions and interests that arise during the discussion and faith-sharing itself.
- Close the discussion and faith-sharing with prayer, about 5–10 minutes. You may use the Closing Prayer at the end of each lesson or one of your choosing at the end of the book. It is important to allow people to pray for personal and community needs and to give thanks for how God is moving in your lives.
- View the wrap-up lecture associated with each lesson (15–20 minutes). You may watch the lecture online, use a DVD, or provide a live lecture by a qualified local speaker. View the lecture together at the end of the session or, if your group runs out of time, you may invite group members to watch the lecture on their own time after the discussion.

A note to individuals

- If you are using this resource for individual study, simply move at your own pace. Take as much time as you need to read, study, and pray with the material.
- If you would like to share this experience with others, consider inviting a friend or family member to join you for your next study. Even a small group of two or three provides an opportunity for fruitful dialog and faith-sharing!

Hebrews

LESSON ONE

Introduction and Hebrews 1–2

Begin your personal study and group discussion with a simple and sincere prayer such as:

Prayer

Lord Jesus, by your death, resurrection, and exaltation, you have freed us from our sins. May our study of Hebrews increase our gratitude for this gift of salvation and inspire in us a desire to share with others your saving love.

Read the Introduction on pages 12–15 and the Bible text of Hebrews 1–2 found in the outside columns of pages 16–21, highlighting what stands out to you.

Read the accompanying commentary to add to your understanding.

Respond to the questions on pages 22–25, Exploring Lesson One.

The Closing Prayer on page 25 is for your personal use and may be used at the end of group discussion.

INTRODUCTION

Among the books of the New Testament, the Letter to the Hebrews stands out for its rhetorical and theological brilliance. It is arguably the greatest Christian sermon ever preached or written. Its author deserves to be revered as the patron saint of preachers. He has presented the essential claim of Christian faith that Christ died for our sins in a persuasive argument with a deep emotional appeal. One way to introduce this book is to describe Hebrews as a sermon in written form, of uncertain origin, intended to encourage perseverance in Christian faith.

A sermon in written form

The author describes his work as a "message of encouragement" (13:22), which most interpreters take to mean a speech or sermon in written form. The only literary features that might qualify Hebrews as a letter or epistle are the travel plans and personal greetings that appear in 13:23-24. These features may have been attached to the sermon as it was sent from one community to another. Or perhaps they were interpolated into the text to promote its association with the corpus of Pauline letters.

Hebrews is no ordinary sermon. Indeed, it is a highly literary and rhetorical sermon that is at once simple and subtle. The basic theological point is simple: Christ is both the perfect sacrifice for sins and the priest who offers himself as a sacrifice. The work's sophisticated use of the Greek language indicates a high level of education on the author's part. As a good preacher, the author interweaves expositions of biblical texts and exhortations to faith and good actions. While he sometimes appears to make a formal delineation between exposition and exhortation, he always joins the two. Exposition leads into exhortation, and exhortation leads to further exposition. He announces his main themes beforehand, repeats keywords, begins and ends units in similar ways (a technique called inclusion), and uses various rhetorical devices (alliteration, arguments "from the lesser to the greater," etc.).

The rhetorical handbooks of the Greco-Roman world distinguished three kinds of speeches: forensic or judicial (used in accusing or defending someone in a legal trial), deliberative (used in persuading a public assembly to take action), and epideictic (used at public memorial occasions to confirm a community's values by praise or blame).

Hebrews best fits the conventions of epideictic rhetoric. It celebrates the greatness of Jesus as the Son of God and as the great high priest, and promotes the values that he stood for. It offers comparisons with the angels, Moses, the priests of the old covenant, and Melchizedek to extol the greatness of Jesus. It praises and blames those who are being addressed and seeks to confirm their positive beliefs in the hope of rousing them from spiritual sluggishness and of rescuing them from the danger of falling away from the Christian faith.

The basic outline of Hebrews is clear enough. The first main part (1:1–4:13) establishes Jesus' superiority as God's Son to the angels and to Moses and uses various biblical texts to explore Jesus' significance and the need for persevering in Christian life. The second main part (4:14–10:18) concerns the high priesthood of Christ and the perfect sacrifice of Christ. The third main part (10:19–13:25) reflects on the nature of Christian life and the need for perseverance and endurance in the face of suffering. There are many much more elaborate outlines. But even the simple tripartite outline is not entirely adequate, since the author is so skilled in making transitions, in anticipating themes to be developed later, and in integrating biblical expositions and exhortations.

Of uncertain origin

The authorship of Hebrews has always been controversial. The early church writer Origen said: "But who wrote the epistle, in truth God knows" (Eusebius, *Ecclesiastical History* 6.25.14). Although the reference to "our brother Timothy" in 13:23 might suggest Pauline authorship, the language, literary style and form, and theology are very different from those of Paul's genuine letters. The attributions to Barnabas (see Acts 4:36) and Apollos (see Acts 18:24) are at best guesses.

The sermon in written form is anonymous. The author never names himself, nor does he reveal much personal information. But some reliable statements can be made about his identity. The author had sophisticated knowledge of the Old Testament in its Greek translation and displays a good familiarity with the techniques of Jewish biblical interpretation. He must have been Jewish. Nevertheless, he was convinced that God had done something so dramatically new and significant through the life, death, resurrection, and exaltation of Jesus that the institutions of the old covenant with Israel through Moses on Mount Sinai were no longer effective. They were only types or shadows of the realities fulfilled in Christ. As he addresses his audience, the author seeks to serve as their teacher and pastoral guide. To respect the mixed genre of Hebrews as a sermon in written form, I refer in the commentary to the author, the writer, and the preacher alternatively, as well as to the readers, the congregation, the community, and the audience.

Those originally addressed in Hebrews seem to have been Jewish Christians who had embraced Christianity with enthusiasm but were wavering and in danger of giving into discouragement and falling away, especially in the face of suffering (see 12:3-11). It is very tempting to locate the community in Rome on the basis of 13:24 ("those from Italy send you greetings") and the earliest attestations of Hebrews in Clement of Rome's first letter to the Corinthians (1 Clement). But there is no certainty here. Neither is the date of composition certain, since practically anytime between A.D. 50 and 100 is possible. The absence of any reference to the destruction of the Jerusalem temple in A.D. 70 might suggest an early date (the fifties or sixties), though one must admit that the author is more interested in explaining Scripture than in commenting on contemporary events. With these cautions in mind, the hypothesis that Hebrews was addressed to a Jewish Christian community at Rome in the late fifties or early sixties of the first century A.D. remains nonetheless the most attractive setting.

Uncertainty also surrounds the history-of-religions background of Hebrews, so much so that this issue is often called "the mystery of Hebrews." Although some of the author's biblical expositions sound something like what one finds in the writings of Philo of Alexandria, he seems more interested in typology than in allegory. The portrayal of Melchizedek as a heavenly figure in some Dead Sea Scrolls was initially thought to illumine Hebrews 7. But it now appears that the author simply gives his own christological readings of the pertinent biblical texts. Concepts that developed in Gnosticism are sometimes read back into Hebrews, but again the results only highlight the author's theological originality. The New Testament document that is closest to Hebrews is 1 Peter. It is a sermon addressed to alienated and suffering Christians, who are urged to find encouragement and hope in the example of Christ the Suffering Servant. While those addressed in 1 Peter were mainly Gentile Christians, the main audience for Hebrews appears to have been Jewish Christians.

To encourage perseverance

Hebrews is a sustained theological reflection on the very early Christian confession of faith that Christ died for us and for our sins. This confession appears both in Paul's writings (see Gal 1:4; 3:13; 2 Cor 5:14, 21; Rom 5:6; 14:15) and in the pre-Pauline creedal formulas that Paul quotes (see 1 Cor 11:24; 15:3; Rom 3:25-26).

The author of Hebrews shares and develops the idea of the sacrificial nature of Christ's death and its atoning value. However, his most distinctive theological contribution is the concept of the high priesthood of Christ. According to early Christian tradition (see Mark 10:45; 14:24; and especially 14:36), Jesus willingly offered himself in death. Since the one who offers a sacrifice is a priest, the author endeavors to show that Christ can be called a priest despite the fact that he was not born into the

Jewish priestly tribe of Levi. The basic theological claim of Hebrews is that Christ is both the perfect sacrifice for sins and the priest who offered himself as that sacrifice.

In developing this thesis, the author assumes that Christ is the key to the Old Testament Scriptures. Not content to leave behind the Old Testament, he argues that the words of Scripture only make sense when attributed to Christ or applied to him. His favorite texts are the royal Psalms 2 and 110, and in his exhortations he calls upon Psalms 8 and 95 among others. The description of the Day of Atonement ritual in Leviticus 16 is the basic source for establishing Christ's sacrifice and priesthood.

The author insists on the superiority of Christ as the Son of God over the angels and over Moses. Because Christ is both the high priest and the perfect sacrifice, his saving action—his death, resurrection, and exaltation taken as a single event—has made possible the forgiveness of sins, confident access to God, and hope for eternal life with God.

The people addressed in Hebrews seem to be having a hard time in accepting the absolute sufficiency of Christ's perfect sacrifice on the cross. If they are to persevere in Christian faith, they need a spiritual renewal. At various points the author addresses their situation directly with stern warnings and words of encouragement. Most of all, he hopes that his biblical-theological presentation of Christ's sacrifice and priesthood will give them the appropriate theological framework to put aside their doubts and spiritual sluggishness and to revitalize their Christian faith and practice.

To that end the author portrays Christ as the pioneer (the one who has already gone before us) and the leader for those who follow him on the way to eternal life with God. The risen and exalted Christ remains a mediator on our behalf in the present (9:24) and will appear again to bring salvation in the future (9:28). His perfect sacrifice renders unnecessary the sacrifices and priests of the old covenant. In fact, these persons and institutions were at best types or signs that have received their full definition in Christ.

Two hard questions

Does Hebrews illumine the Christian priesthood? The work is mainly concerned with the priesthood of the Old Testament and the priesthood of Christ. It does not speak directly about the communal priesthood of all Christians (see 1 Pet 2:9; Rev 1:6; 5:10; 20:6) or about the Christian ministerial priesthood. However, many Christians have found in Christ's priesthood an apt metaphor for describing Christian life in general. It has also been traditional among Catholics and other Christians to find in Christ's priesthood the model and dynamism for the ministerial priesthood. But some Protestants regard Christ's priesthood to be the end of all claims to priesthood, since his perfect "once for all" (Heb 10:10) sacrifice has rendered unnecessary all other sacrifices and priesthoods. The problem is that Hebrews is silent on this important question and can be (and has been) read as supporting or denying all the various positions about priesthood.

Is Hebrews anti-Jewish? Since both the author and his audience seem to have been Jews, such a charge seems unfair and anachronistic. In fact, Hebrews is an interpretation of Judaism in the light of Christ. Without the authoritative Scriptures of Israel and the great heroes and institutions of the biblical tradition, there would be little substance to Hebrews. And yet perhaps more than any other New Testament writer, the author of Hebrews insists that the old covenant, priesthood, and sacrificial system have been superseded through Christ. Modern Christian readers need to respect the historical (Jewish) setting of Hebrews and to be sensitive to the anti-Jewish potential of the text when it is taken out of its first-century Jewish Christian context.

Another challenge raised by our study is the absence of any direct reference to the **Eucharist** in Hebrews. While other New Testament books clearly point to the connection between Jesus' sacrificial death and the Eucharist (e.g., Luke 22:19; 1 Cor 11:24-26), Hebrews does not mention it. However, this silence need not be interpreted as disagreement. Our belief that eucharistic celebrations are an ongoing participation in the once-for-all, eternal sacrifice of Jesus, the heavenly high priest, is fully compatible with the text of Hebrews.

Reading Hebrews

Hebrews is a sermon in written form. It presents a sustained theological argument, and so it may be helpful to read it straight through at one sitting. Its rhetoric and theology are highly sophisticated and difficult for modern readers, and therefore it deserves careful study, with the commentary that follows as a guide. It may be helpful to look up the Old Testament texts that the author quotes in order to appreciate how he handles these texts from his christological perspective. One must be aware, however, that the author used the ancient Greek version (Septuagint) of the Old Testament, which often differs from the Hebrew text on which our modern translations are based. A communal reading of this sermon in written form might serve as a final exercise. A well-prepared and reverent group reading of the whole text takes about fifty minutes. The exercise will help those who have worked through this difficult text to appreciate better the truth of the author's own comment: "The word of God is living and effective, sharper than any two-edged sword" (4:12).

I: Introduction

CHAPTER 1

1In times past, God spoke in partial and various
ways to our ancestors through the prophets; 2in
these last days, he spoke to us through a son,
whom he made heir of all things and through
whom he created the universe,

3who is the refulgence of his glory,
the very imprint of his being,
and who sustains all things by his mighty
word.
When he had accomplished purification
from sins,
he took his seat at the right hand of the
Majesty on high,
4as far superior to the angels
as the name he has inherited is more
excellent than theirs.

continue

GOD'S SON AND GOD'S WORD

Heb 1:1–4:13

1:1-4 Prologue: Jesus as the climax of divine revelation

The prologue serves as an introduction or overture to the entire sermon by calling attention to major themes and to the pivotal place of Jesus in the history of salvation. Using the rhetorical device of alliteration, in which several words begin with the same letter ("past . . . partial . . . prophets"), the author begins in 1:1-2a by showing how Jesus continues the story of God's communication to Israel and brings it to a definitive point or climax. He develops the idea by four contrasts: (1) Whereas God spoke "in times past," now he has spoken "in these last days" (the new era ushered in by Jesus and issuing in the fullness of God's kingdom). (2) Whereas God spoke "to our ancestors" (historic Israel), now he has spoken "to us" (the Christian community). (3) Whereas God spoke "through the prophets" (including Moses, Joshua, and David, as well as those known traditionally as the prophets), now he has spoken through "a son" (Jesus). (4) Whereas God spoke "in partial and various ways," now he has spoken in a full and definitive way (through Jesus).

In describing the person and work of Jesus in 1:2b-3, the author highlights his identity as the Messiah and as Wisdom. Jesus' identity as the Messiah is developed with the help of two psalms (2 and 110) that serve as major texts throughout the sermon. Both psalms originated in the ritual associated with the coronation of kings in ancient Israel. The king was "anointed" as part of his coronation, and the word "Messiah" means "the anointed one." By declaring Jesus as "heir of all things" (see Ps 2:8) and as taking his seat at God's right hand (Ps 110:1), the author tells us right away that Jesus is the Messiah of Jewish expectations. What historic Israel hoped from its kings, Jesus has provided.

Jesus' identity as the Wisdom of God is established by evoking terms and motifs from various Old Testament passages in which Wisdom is portrayed as the agent of God in creation (see Proverbs 8, Sirach 24, and Wisdom 7). The author affirms that Jesus was God's agent in creating the universe ("through whom he created the universe," see Prov 8:30; Wis 7:22), that he reflects God's glory and represents God's being (see Wis 7:26), and that he carries on God's work of creation ("who sustains all things"). The motif of Jesus as the Wisdom of God is prominent in early Christian hymns preserved in other New Testament books, most notably Colossians 1:15-20 and John 1:1-18.

While identifying Jesus as God's Messiah and Wisdom, the author also introduces his major theme of Jesus' role in the "purification from sins," a work accomplished through his sacrificial death on the cross and his subsequent exaltation to the heavenly throne of God. Likewise, in 1:4 he announces the theme that will be developed in what follows immediately: the superiority of Jesus to the angels. This theme is related to the superior "name" that Jesus bears as the Son of God. The author's task will be to show why the Son should be regarded as superior to the angels.

1:5-14 Jesus as superior to the angels

Why the author felt compelled to take on this task is not certain. There is some evidence in the Dead Sea Scrolls and other early Jewish texts for veneration of angels. And some early Christians may have regarded Jesus as an angel. Or the issue may have been entirely theoretical.

The device that the author uses to establish Jesus' superiority to the angels is a chain (or *catena*) of biblical quotations. While the *catena* genre was used by Jewish writers of the times, the author of Hebrews makes it serve his christological purpose. For him, Christ is the key to the Scriptures, and so all the biblical texts that he quotes are assumed to speak to or about Christ. There are three pairs of quotations (Heb 1:5, 6-7, 8-12), along with a single quotation of Psalm 110:1 (Heb 1:13).

The introduction to the *catena* in 1:5a ("to which of the angels did God ever say") establishes that the purpose is to prove the superiority of the Son. The concluding comment in 1:14 about the angels as servants is a case of inclusion, in which an argument is begun and ended in similar ways.

II: The Son Higher than the Angels

Messianic Enthronement

5 For to which of the angels did God ever say:

"You are my son; this day I have begotten you"?

Or again:

"I will be a father to him, and he shall be a
son to me"?

6 And again, when he leads the first-born into the world, he says:

"Let all the angels of God worship him."

7 Of the angels he says:

"He makes his angels winds
and his ministers a fiery flame";

8 but of the Son:

"Your throne, O God, stands forever and ever;

continue

Early Jewish Christians who read or heard Hebrews were familiar with **angels in their usual biblical roles** as God's messengers and agents on earth. Over time, the functions performed by angels in Scripture increased: some were said to serve as the patrons of nations (Dan 10:20-21), others as the rulers of the elements and heavenly bodies (Judg 5:20; Ps 104:4).

Of particular relevance to the book of Hebrews was the role assumed by one angel in particular, the archangel Michael, who, according to certain Jewish texts, performed priestly functions in the heavenly sanctuary (see 3 Enoch 38–40). Hebrews' contention that it is Jesus—and not some angelic minister—who presides in the heavenly sanctuary may help explain why the text is so clear that Jesus is superior to the angels (1:5-14).

and a righteous scepter is the scepter of
your kingdom.
9You loved justice and hated wickedness;
therefore God, your God, anointed you
with the oil of gladness above your
companions";

10and:

"At the beginning, O Lord, you established
the earth,
and the heavens are the works of your
hands.
11They will perish, but you remain;
and they will all grow old like a garment.
12You will roll them up like a cloak,
and like a garment they will be changed.
But you are the same, and your years will
have no end."

13But to which of the angels has he ever said:

"Sit at my right hand
until I make your enemies your
footstool"?

14Are they not all ministering spirits sent to serve, for the sake of those who are to inherit salvation?

continue

In 1:5 the first pair of quotations—Psalm 2:7 and 2 Samuel 7:14—serve to identify Jesus as God's Son and Messiah: "You are my son . . . he shall be a son to me." The assumption is that God is the speaker and addresses Jesus as his Messiah/Son. Part of the ideology of kingship in ancient Israel was that the king became God's "son" at his accession to the throne. And so when applied to Jesus, the terms "Messiah" and "Son" are synonyms.

In 1:6-7 the second pair of quotations—Deuteronomy 32:43/Psalm 97:7 and Psalm 104:4—establish the inferiority of the angels to the Son of God. The assumption is that God spoke these words when Jesus the Wisdom of God took on human flesh ("when he leads the first-born into the world") and that these words concern the Son of God. The first text says that the role of the angels is to worship the Son, and the second text presents the angels as instruments of God ("winds . . . a fiery flame").

In 1:8-12 the third pair of quotations—Psalm 45:7-8 and Psalm 102:26-28—takes texts originally addressed to God and applies them to the Messiah/Son ("your throne, O God . . . O Lord, you established"). The emphasis is on the eternity of Jesus' reign as God's Messiah/Son ("forever and ever . . . God, your God, anointed you . . . your years will have no end"). While such things cannot be said of angels, applying these biblical affirmations about God to Christ suggests his own authority, eternity, and even divinity.

In 1:13 the final (single) quotation—Psalm 110:1—applies what was said by God to the king at his coronation ("sit at my right hand / until I make your enemies your footstool") to the resurrected and exalted Messiah/Son. Throughout Hebrews, the center of attention will be Jesus' death, resurrection, and exaltation understood as one great event. The *catena* concludes in 1:14 with a comment about the role of the angels as servants of God ("ministering spirits") on behalf of all those who seek salvation.

2:1-4 A call to commitment and responsibility

At many points in his sermon the author addresses his audience directly and challenges them to apply his message about Christ to their own situation. Even in his exhortations, however, he injects new theological considerations based on the Old Testament and on God's saving activity in Jesus.

As a good preacher, the author moves in 2:1 from the *catena* of biblical quotations to their significance for Christian life and includes himself among those being addressed ("therefore we must attend . . ."). The expression "what we have heard" may refer to the gospel message in general, to the biblical passages applied to Christ in 1:5-14, or to Jesus as the Word of God—or all three at once. The danger that the audience faces is expressed by the phrase "so that we may not be carried away," which evokes the image of a ship failing to reach its harbor safely. The author fears that his people may drift away from the gospel that they had once embraced.

The warning in 2:2-3a builds on the case developed about the Son's superiority to the angels. It employs the rhetorical device of arguing "from the lesser to the greater" and assumes that the law was given to Moses on Sinai through the mediation of angels (see Acts 7:53; Gal 3:19). If the Mosaic Law given through angels punishes each and every transgression, how much more will God punish neglect of the salvation given through Christ. The logic is that the greater revelation (the gospel) given through the greater revealer (Christ) will exact greater punishment from those who fail to attend to it.

Arguing **"from the lesser to the greater"** (*a minori ad maius*), as in Hebrews 2:2-3, was a common rhetorical strategy in rabbinic exegesis and is used throughout Hebrews. (See 7:21-22; 9:13-14; 10:28-29; 12:25.)

CHAPTER 2

Exhortation to Faithfulness

1Therefore, we must attend all the more to what
we have heard, so that we may not be carried away.
2For if the word announced through angels proved
firm, and every transgression and disobedience
received its just recompense, 3how shall we escape
if we ignore so great a salvation? Announced origi-
nally through the Lord, it was confirmed for us by
those who had heard. 4God added his testimony
by signs, wonders, various acts of power, and dis-
tribution of the gifts of the holy Spirit according
to his will.

Exaltation through Abasement

5For it was not to angels that he subjected the
world to come, of which we are speaking. 6Instead,
someone has testified somewhere:

"What is man that you are mindful of him,
or the son of man that you care for him?

continue

Having raised the threat of severe punishment, the author in 2:3b-4 reminds his audience about the nature of the salvation brought by Christ. It was announced by Jesus ("the Lord") and confirmed by the apostolic witnesses and by God through miracles ("signs, wonders, various acts of power") and through the gifts of the holy Spirit (not a major figure in Hebrews). Note the "trinitarian" dimension that serves as the framework for describing the saving work of Christ.

2:5-9 Jesus as the Son of Man

Having reflected on the significance of the salvation brought by Jesus for the community of faith, the author takes up again the theme of Jesus' superiority to the angels. According to a biblical tradition (see Deut 32:8; Dan 10:20-21; 12:1), God placed the world in the present age under the governance of angels. According to early Christian faith, however, the new age or "world to come" (2:5) has already been inaugurated in and through Christ. But the quotation of Psalm 110:1 in Hebrews 1:13 ("until I make your enemies your footstool") could give the impression that Christ's reign was still future. And so the author contends that Christ's reign is both present and future and that it began with Jesus' incarnation, death, and exaltation.

The biblical vehicle for the author's argument is Psalm 8:5-7, which is part of a meditation on the great dignity of human beings. The psalmist (the "someone [who] has testified somewhere") praises God ("you") for God's care and love for humankind ("man . . . the son of man") and observes that God has placed human beings a little lower than the angels and given them stewardship over the world (see Gen 1:26, 28).

[7]You made him for a little while lower than
the angels;
you crowned him with glory and honor,
[8]subjecting all things under his feet."

In "subjecting" all things [to him], he left nothing
not "subject to him." Yet at present we do not see
"all things subject to him," [9]but we do see Jesus
"crowned with glory and honor" because he suf-
fered death, he who "for a little while" was made
"lower than the angels," that by the grace of God
he might taste death for everyone.

[10]For it was fitting that he, for whom and
through whom all things exist, in bringing many
children to glory, should make the leader to their
salvation perfect through suffering. [11]He who
consecrates and those who are being consecrated
all have one origin. Therefore, he is not ashamed
to call them "brothers," [12]saying:

"I will proclaim your name to my brothers,
in the midst of the assembly I will praise
you";

[13]and again:

"I will put my trust in him";

and again:

"Behold, I and the children God has given me."

[14]Now since the children share in blood and flesh,
he likewise shared in them, that through death he
might destroy the one who has the power of death,
that is, the devil, [15]and free those who through fear
of death had been subject to slavery all their life.
[16]Surely he did not help angels but rather the de-
scendants of Abraham; [17]therefore, he had to be-
come like his brothers in every way, that he might
be a merciful and faithful high priest before God
to expiate the sins of the people. [18]Because he him-
self was tested through what he suffered, he is able
to help those who are being tested.

True to his interpretive principle that Christ is the key to the Scriptures, the author assumes that Psalm 8 speaks about Christ as the "son of man." In his interpretation (2:8b-9), he affirms that God has already placed all creation under the governance of Christ as the Son of Man. The problem is that humans do not yet perceive Christ's sovereignty, though they surely will do so in the fullness of God's kingdom. What is now perceived through faith is the risen and exalted Christ ("crowned . . . with glory and honor"). His glorification followed from his suffering and death, when he was lower than the angels "for a little while." The paradox is that Christ's humiliation in his passion became the occasion for the exaltation of us all. The idea that Christ's death was the perfect sacrifice for sins and opened up the possibility for the salvation of all humans is introduced by the concluding clause: "that by the grace of God he might taste death for everyone" (2:9).

The paradoxical association of **Christ's death on the cross** with his being "crowned with glory and honor" (2:9) is a common motif in the Gospel of John, where Jesus himself speaks of the crucifixion as a moment of glorification when he will be exalted ("lifted up") and will draw everyone to himself (John 3:14; 12:32).

2:10-18 Christ in solidarity with humans

The fundamental affirmation of Hebrews is expressed in 2:10: God ("for whom and through whom all things exist") made Jesus the pioneer or champion ("leader") to bring all humans to salvation, and the way by which this goal was achieved was through the cross, on which Christ was made "perfect through suffering." This statement captures the self-sacrifice involved in Jesus' death on the cross as well as the atoning value of his death for others. Thus Jesus can be understood (as we will see) as both the priest (because he offered himself willingly) and the sacrifice (because his death was for us and for our sins).

Jesus' solidarity with humans and his special relationship with God are established in 2:11-13 by a series of Old Testament quotations. Both Christ ("he who consecrates") and humans ("those who are being consecrated") share a common origin in God and in humanity. And so Christ can call other humans "brothers." The first biblical quotation is Psalm 22:22—from the prayer of the righteous sufferer, which is also the source of Jesus' last words on the cross, according to Mark (15:34) and Matthew (27:46). In the author's christological framework, Jesus ("I") confesses and praises God ("you") among his fellow humans ("to my brothers"). In the second biblical quotation (Isa 8:17-18), Christ ("I") professes trust in God ("in him") and identifies himself with other humans ("I and the children God has given me"). Thus Christ is the link or mediator between God and humans.

The classic question, Why did Christ become human? is taken up in 2:14-18. By sharing our humanity, Christ was able to render inoperative the devil as the one who has power over death and to free us from the fear of death that makes us slaves (2:14-15). The object of Christ's saving work was the "descendants of Abraham," which includes not only Israel as the chosen people of God but also the many nations of which Abraham was the father (2:16). Only by being fully human could Christ be both our priest ("a merciful and faithful high priest") and our sacrifice ("to expiate the sins of the people"). Only by being tested through suffering could Christ help us as we are being tested. These ideas about the priesthood of Christ will be developed at great length in chapters 5–10.

EXPLORING LESSON ONE

1. According to the Introduction, what is the "basic theological point" of the book of Hebrews?

2. Hebrews is described as a highly "rhetorical" text. This means it is particularly effective or persuasive in communicating its message. What are some of the rhetorical devices or techniques its author uses?

3. a) Why can we presume that the author of Hebrews was Jewish?

   b) Who was likely the original audience for Hebrews?

4. How would you respond to the question of whether Hebrews is anti-Semitic (anti-Jewish)?

5. Hebrews indicates that in Jesus, God has brought divine communication with Israel to its climax (1:1-4). What four contrasts does the author use to explain this?

6. Hebrews challenges its readers to concentrate on the message of salvation they have received, lest they be "carried away" (2:1). What worldly distractions tempt you away from your faith and your commitments to prayer and serving others? How do you combat such temptations?

7. a) It is clear from its numerous Old Testament references that Hebrews understands Christ as the key to understanding Scripture. What reason is there for interpreting the Old Testament in this way? (See Luke 24:25-27.)

b) What danger might there be in always interpreting the Old Testament in light of the New Testament?

8. What is paradoxical about Jesus' death as explained in Hebrews 2:8-9? (See also John 12:32-33; Phil 2:8-9; Col 2:14-15.)

9. a) How does Hebrews establish Christ's solidarity with humanity (2:10-14, 17-18)?

b) Based on what you know about the life of Jesus, does this description ring true for you? What incident from Jesus' life helps you relate to him as a human being?

10. What is most attractive to you about the book of Hebrews so far? What do you think you will find challenging as you continue your study?

CLOSING PRAYER

Prayer

Because he himself was tested through what he suffered, he is able to help those who are being tested. (Heb 2:18)

Lord Jesus, through the miracle and gift of your Incarnation, you experienced firsthand the trials of human life. Support us with your compassionate love so we may overcome the hardships we encounter, knowing you are with us. We pray today especially for . . .

LESSON TWO

Hebrews 3:1–5:10

Begin your personal study and group discussion with a simple and sincere prayer such as:

Prayer

Lord Jesus, by your death, resurrection, and exaltation, you have freed us from our sins. May our study of Hebrews increase our gratitude for this gift of salvation and inspire in us a desire to share with others your saving love.

Read the Bible text of Hebrews 3:1–5:10 found in the outside columns of pages 28–34, highlighting what stands out to you.

Read the accompanying commentary to add to your understanding.

Respond to the questions on pages 35–37, Exploring Lesson Two.

The Closing Prayer on page 38 is for your personal use and may be used at the end of group discussion.

III: Jesus, Faithful and Compassionate High Priest

CHAPTER 3

Jesus, Superior to Moses

1 Therefore, holy "brothers," sharing in a heav-
enly calling, reflect on Jesus, the apostle and high
priest of our confession, 2 who was faithful to the
one who appointed him, just as Moses was "faith-
ful in [all] his house." 3 But he is worthy of more
"glory" than Moses, as the founder of a house has
more "honor" than the house itself. 4 Every house
is founded by someone, but the founder of all is
God. 5 Moses was "faithful in all his house" as a
"servant" to testify to what would be spoken, 6 but
Christ was faithful as a son placed over his house.
We are his house, if [only] we hold fast to our
confidence and pride in our hope.

Israel's Infidelity a Warning

7 Therefore, as the holy Spirit says:
"Oh, that today you would hear his voice,
8 'Harden not your hearts as at the rebellion
in the day of testing in the desert,
9 where your ancestors tested and tried me
and saw my works 10 for forty years.
Because of this I was provoked with that
generation

continue

3:1-6 Jesus as superior to Moses

The preacher returns in 3:1 to direct address. He reminds his congregation that as "brothers" of Christ and of one another, they share in the holiness that reflects God, the holy one par excellence, and in the call to eternal life with God. Identifying Jesus as "the apostle" (the one "sent" from God—the only New Testament application of this title to Christ) and "high priest" (a title already introduced in 2:17 and soon to become the center of attention), the author in 3:2 focuses on Jesus' fidelity to God as "the one who appointed him." He also introduces the figure of Moses and the characterization of Moses as "faithful in all his house."

This description of Moses comes from Numbers 12:7(8): "Not so with my servant Moses! / Throughout my house he is worthy of trust." In the Old Testament context, Moses appears as the instrument of God's revelation who is superior to Aaron, Miriam, and all other recipients of divine revelation. The "house" is Israel as the people of God, where Moses functioned as the "servant" of God.

In comparing Moses and Christ in 3:3-6, the author is more concerned to praise Christ than to denigrate Moses. He proceeds on two fronts: the house (3:3-4) and the servant (3:5-6). Just as the architect-builder of a house deserves more praise than the house itself, so God (and Christ as God's agent) deserves more praise than Moses in founding the people of God. Just as in a large household a son is more important than a servant, so Christ the Son is more important than Moses the servant in the people of God. Whereas Moses was a servant "in" God's house, Christ was a son placed "over" the house. Thus Jesus' faithfulness as God's Son was superior to the faithfulness of God's servant Moses.

Hebrews' **comparison between Moses and Jesus** (3:1-6) is implicit elsewhere in the New Testament. In the Sermon on the Mount, for example, Jesus offers extended interpretations of the laws of Moses (Matt 5:21-48), and in the Gospel of John, the Mosaic law is compared to the "grace and truth [which] came through Jesus Christ" (John 1:17; see also John 3:14; 6:32-33; 9:28-29).

The preacher concludes in 3:6b by identifying the Christian community as the "house" or people of God ("we are his house") and by warning the community to retain their confidence and pride in what God has done and continues to do for them through Christ the Son. Otherwise they may cease to be God's house.

3:7-19 The negative example of Israel in the wilderness

A good preacher frequently offers a congregation positive examples to imitate and negative examples to avoid. As a way of challenging the congregation to emulate the fidelity displayed by Christ, the author presents the negative example of ancient Israel wandering in the wilderness between the Exodus from Egypt and the entrance into the land of Canaan.

The main biblical text is Psalm 95:7b-11 (which is read in light of Numbers 14). The text is introduced as having logical significance ("therefore") and as being from God ("as the holy Spirit says"). In Psalm 95 the admonition to be faithful follows an invitation to worship God, most obviously at the Jerusalem temple (Ps 95:1-7a). The admonition itself recalls the episode of Israel's rebellion in the wilderness (see Exod 17:1-17; Num 14:21-23). The place in which the rebellion took place was called in Hebrew "Massah" (meaning "testing") and "Meribah" (meaning "quarreling"). The text begins with a call to hear God's voice "today" (Heb 3:7b = Ps 95:7b). Then there is a warning to avoid the rebelliousness displayed by the Exodus generation in the wilderness for forty

> and I said, "They have always been of
> erring heart,
> and they do not know my ways."
> [11]As I swore in my wrath,
> "They shall not enter into my rest."'"
>
> [12]Take care, brothers, that none of you may have
> an evil and unfaithful heart, so as to forsake the
> living God. [13]Encourage yourselves daily while it
> is still "today," so that none of you may grow hard-
> ened by the deceit of sin. [14]We have become part-
> ners of Christ if only we hold the beginning of
> the reality firm until the end, [15]for it is said:
>
> "Oh, that today you would hear his voice:
> 'Harden not your hearts as at the rebellion.'"
>
> [16]Who were those who rebelled when they heard?
> Was it not all those who came out of Egypt under
> Moses? [17]With whom was he "provoked for forty
> years"? Was it not those who had sinned, whose
> corpses fell in the desert? [18]And to whom did he
> "swear that they should not enter into his rest," if
> not to those who were disobedient? [19]And we see
> that they could not enter for lack of faith.
>
> *continue*

years (Heb 3:8-9 = Ps 95:8-9). Finally, God recalls his anger at that generation and his resolve that they would not find "rest" in the land of Canaan (Heb 3:10-11 = Ps 95:10-11).

The call to "hold fast" to the hope of salvation and remain firm in faith until the end (3:6-14) is a common theme in New Testament texts. Because the early church faced persecution, **perseverance** was necessary, as reflected in the many exhortations toward watchfulness (e.g., Mark 13:9, 23, 33), and warnings to making the best use of the time one has (the "today" of Heb 3:13; see Luke 13:3-5; John 9:4). Underlying all of this is the understanding that only "the one who perseveres to the end will be saved" (Matt 24:13).

CHAPTER 4

The Sabbath Rest

[1]Therefore, let us be on our guard while the promise of entering into his rest remains, that none of you seem to have failed. [2]For in fact we have received the good news just as they did. But the word that they heard did not profit them, for they were not united in faith with those who listened. [3]For we who believed enter into [that] rest, just as he has said:

"As I swore in my wrath,
'They shall not enter into my rest,'"

and yet his works were accomplished at the foundation of the world. [4]For he has spoken somewhere about the seventh day in this manner, "And God rested on the seventh day from all his works"; [5]and again, in the previously mentioned place, "They shall not enter into my rest." [6]Therefore, since it remains that some will enter into it, and those who formerly received the good news did not enter because of disobedience, [7]he once more set a day, "today," when long afterwards he spoke through David, as already quoted:

"Oh, that today you would hear his voice:
'Harden not your hearts.'"

continue

Having quoted this biblical text at length, the author in 3:12-15 makes an application to the situation of his audience in the first century A.D. First, in 3:12 he warns them against falling away from the living God, as the Exodus generation did, through "an evil and unfaithful heart." Then, in 3:13 he encourages them to regard every day as "today" and not to allow their hearts to be hardened. Finally, in 3:14-15 he warns them again that their partnership with Christ depends on remaining faithful "until the end." The final warning and the application in general are underscored by a repetition of Psalm 95:7b-8 and the key words ("today . . . hear his voice . . . harden not your hearts . . . rebellion").

The application is an example of the actualization of Scripture. Just as the psalmist used the negative example of the Exodus generation to motivate people in his own generation, so the author of Hebrews applies both the example and the biblical text to early Christians in his own day. This process of actualization is carried on whenever the letter to the Hebrews is proclaimed today, since "the word of God is living and effective" (4:12).

Still another rhetorical device in the preacher's repertoire is his use of rhetorical questions. From what had been said and from the way in which the questions are asked, it is clear what answers the preacher expects. The first two questions (3:16 and 3:17) are answered by two more questions, while the final question (3:18) receives a response by means of a declarative sentence (3:19).

The first pair of questions (3:16) establish that those who had rebelled were those Israelites who came out of Egypt with Moses. Their disobedience is the main topic in Psalm 95:7b-11. The second pair of questions (3:17) indicate that God was angry with those people because they sinned in putting God to the test and in rebelling against God. The punishment for that generation's rebelliousness was death in the wilderness before any could enter "rest" in the land of Canaan (see Num 14:29-30).

The third question (3:18) affirms that God swore an oath against the disobedient Israelites, so that they could not enter his rest. And the concluding comment (3:19) attributes their failure to "lack of faith." The author has made two important rhetorical moves here. He has linked disobedience to lack of faith as effect and cause (see Num 14:22-23). And he has repeated the word "rest" several times, thus preparing the listener to ask whether it may refer to something beyond life in the land of Canaan.

4:1-13 The abiding promise of sabbath rest

Having explained Psalm 95:7b-11 in terms of the disobedience and lack of faith shown by the Exodus generation, the preacher in 4:1-2 moves to the congregation that he addresses ("Therefore, let us . . .") and tells them that

God's promise of entering "rest" remains a possibility in the present. He warns them to be on guard lest they fail to have that promise brought to fulfillment. Like the Exodus generation, they have received the "good news" (the same word as "gospel"). Like the Exodus generation, they run the risk of failure if they do not respond in faith. What they should learn from the negative example of the Exodus generation is the pivotal importance of faith resulting in obedience. Only then can they hope to enjoy the "rest" that God has promised.

What is this "rest"? It is not simply life in the land of Canaan after the Exodus from Egypt. Indeed, it remains a present possibility for the early Christians as God's people ("we who believed"). To clarify the meaning of "rest," the author in 4:3-5 uses the Jewish interpretive technique of explaining one verse in Scripture by referring to another verse, which is linked to the first verse by a common word. Part of the author's main text has been Psalm 95:11: "As I swore in my wrath, / 'They shall not enter into my rest.'" Genesis 2:2 is another text that mentions "rest": "And God rested on the seventh day from all his works." The second text, of course, is from the biblical account of creation and expresses God's plan for creation. The combination of the two texts suggests that "rest" really refers to eternal life with God. The "rest" denied the Exodus generation was but a shadow of the rest that God has enjoyed since the beginning of creation and that God makes available to all who believe.

In 4:6-8 the author makes clear that God's promise of rest remains valid, despite the failure of the Exodus generation to attain it because of their disobedience. The key word in this section is "today," which suggests that God's promise of rest remains a possibility even after the Exodus generation. Here the author works with the traditional ascription of the psalms to David (see 4:7). Now David lived long after Joshua, the one who finally did lead God's people into the promised land of Canaan. If Joshua had given genuine rest to God's people, David would not have been able to speak about "today" as the time to hear God's voice and so enjoy rest with God. In Greek the names Joshua and Jesus are the same. But the rest that God's people enjoyed under Joshua's leadership was but a shadow or type of the genuine rest that is now available to God's people through Jesus' leadership.

Finally, in 4:9-10 the author brings together what he has been saying about rest: "a sabbath rest still remains for the people of God" (4:9). This sabbath rest is God's own sabbath rest on the seventh day of creation (see Gen 2:2); it is not simply life in the land of Canaan or even observance of the sabbath day. Rather, it is sharing in God's sabbath rest, which began on the seventh day of creation and lasts forever. It is fullness of life with God.

8 Now if Joshua had given them rest, he would not
have spoken afterwards of another day. 9 Therefore,
a sabbath rest still remains for the people of God.
10 And whoever enters into God's rest, rests from
his own works as God did from his. 11 Therefore,
let us strive to enter into that rest, so that no one
may fall after the same example of disobedience.
12 Indeed, the word of God is living and effective,
sharper than any two-edged sword, penetrating
even between soul and spirit, joints and marrow,
and able to discern reflections and thoughts of the
heart. 13 No creature is concealed from him, but
everything is naked and exposed to the eyes of him
to whom we must render an account.

continue

The **Sabbath** in Scripture is a day of rest, the seventh day of creation (Gen 2:2-3). Originally, Christians (many of whom were Jews) observed the traditional Jewish Sabbath on Saturday but also commemorated Sunday as the "day of the Lord"—the day Jesus rose from the dead. In time, Sunday became the Christian Sabbath, with all the customs associated with a feast day or a day abstaining from work.

Jesus, Compassionate High Priest

[14]Therefore, since we have a great high priest who has passed through the heavens, Jesus, the Son of God, let us hold fast to our confession. [15]For we do not have a high priest who is unable to sympathize with our weaknesses, but one who has similarly been tested in every way, yet without sin. [16]So let us confidently approach the throne of grace to receive mercy and to find grace for timely help.

continue

The metaphor that likens God's word to a **"two-edged sword"** (4:12) may have been influenced by Isaiah 49:2, where the servant of the Lord speaks God's word with a "mouth like a sharp-edged sword." Another possible source is Wisdom 18:15-16, where God's "all-powerful word" is likened to "a fierce warrior bearing the sharp sword of [God's] inexorable decree." The image resurfaces in Revelation 1:16, where "one like a son of man" appears with "a sharp two-edged sword" coming out of his mouth.

And yet, as 4:11 makes clear, the enjoyment of God's own rest demands a deliberate choice ("let us strive to enter into that rest") to avoid the kind of disobedience displayed by the Exodus generation ("so that no one may fall").

The preacher ends the first main part of his sermon in 4:12-13 with reflections on the word of God and the omniscience of God. The word of God (4:12) is more than the book we call the Bible. Because it comes from the living God, the word of God is living and active. Throughout his sermon thus far, the preacher has been concerned to show that the Scriptures can speak effectively to people in his own time. They are not simply witnesses to the past but rather have significance for "today." So effective are the Scriptures in addressing the concerns of people today that they can be compared to a sharp ("two-edged") sword that can penetrate into a person's inmost self ("between soul and spirit, joints and marrow") and can distinguish among thoughts and intentions.

In 4:13 the subject changes from the word of God to God ("him"), or more precisely, to the omniscience of God. Nothing can remain hidden from God. And to God everyone must be ready to render an accounting, as to a judge. Thus the author seeks to motivate his congregation to strive ever more vigorously for eternal life with God ("rest") by reminding them of the possible consequences of not doing so.

THE PRIESTHOOD AND SACRIFICE OF CHRIST

Heb 4:14–10:18

4:14–5:10 Jesus as the compassionate high priest

The author began his sermon by establishing Jesus' identity as the Son of God. In the central section of his sermon, he will show how the Son of God is also the great high priest. The material in 4:14-16 serves as the link between the first two main sections, and enables the preacher to advance his argument about the saving significance of Jesus' death and resurrection. The reuse of many of the same words and ideas in 10:19-23 will in turn enable him to round off (by the device of inclusion) the second part and move to the third and final part.

True to his craft as a preacher, the author in 4:14-16 alternates between theological statements about Jesus' high priesthood (4:14a, 15) and exhortations ("let us . . . ," 4:14b, 16). The first theological statement (4:14a) must be understood against the background of the Jewish Day of Atonement ritual described in Leviticus 16. There the Jewish high priest is instructed to pass through the curtain in front of the Holy of Holies and to offer sacrifice on behalf of the sins of the people. But Jesus the Son of God "has passed through the heavens" in his resurrection and exaltation. Whereas the Jewish high priest entered only the earthly symbol of God's presence, Jesus has entered the real abode of God (heaven). More than anyone else, therefore, Jesus deserves the title of "great high priest." The first exhortation (4:14b) concerns perseverance in the confession of faith in the saving significance of Jesus' death for us and for our sins.

While the details associated with the **Day of Atonement** are fully described in Leviticus 16, the reason for the ritual is found in God's desire to provide a path for sinners to be restored to a right relationship with God. God takes "no pleasure in the death of the wicked" but only wills that the wicked "turn from their ways and live" (Ezek 33:11). In Jesus, Christians believe that God's compassionate mercy has provided the perfect means of reconciliation and salvation.

CHAPTER 5

1 Every high priest is taken from among men
and made their representative before God, to offer
gifts and sacrifices for sins. 2 He is able to deal pa-
tiently with the ignorant and erring, for he him-
self is beset by weakness 3 and so, for this reason,
must make sin offerings for himself as well as for
the people. 4 No one takes this honor upon himself
but only when called by God, just as Aaron was.
5 In the same way, it was not Christ who glorified
himself in becoming high priest, but rather the
one who said to him:

"You are my son;
this day I have begotten you";

6 just as he says in another place:

"You are a priest forever
according to the order of Melchizedek."

7 In the days when he was in the flesh, he offered
prayers and supplications with loud cries and tears
to the one who was able to save him from death,
and he was heard because of his reverence. 8 Son
though he was, he learned obedience from what
he suffered; 9 and when he was made perfect, he
became the source of eternal salvation for all who
obey him, 10 declared by God high priest according
to the order of Melchizedek.

The second theological statement (4:15) again takes as its premise an idea in Leviticus 16—that the high priest is a sinner and makes atonement for his own sins. Though Jesus was "without sin," he nonetheless experienced the moral and physical testing (see Mark 1:12-13; Matt 4:1-11; Luke 4:1-13) that is part of the human condition. As fully human, the Son of God can "sympathize with our weaknesses." The second exhortation (4:16) moves beyond "holding fast" and urges the readers to approach God's throne with boldness. This confidence is based on the new relationship made possible through Jesus' activity as our "great high priest" in his sacrificial death and exaltation. While the motif of God's throne might imply judgment and condemnation, now through Christ it has become a "throne of grace" (a place of divine favor) from which one can expect mercy and grace from God. It is Christ who makes possible this access to God's throne and this confident attitude among those who approach God.

But how can Jesus of Nazareth be called a high priest at all? In ancient Israel only men from the tribe of Levi who could trace their heritage back to Aaron were qualified to serve as high priests. As the author freely admits in 7:14, Jesus was descended from Judah and so had no earthly claim to the Jewish priesthood. The answer to the question resides in the different qualifications for priesthood developed in 5:1-10 and in the different priesthood explained in 7:1-28. (Note the reuse of terms from 5:1-3 in 7:27-28.) The intervening exhortation in 5:11–6:20 spells out the consequences of Jesus' different high priesthood for Christian life.

The high priest is first of all (5:1) a mediator between God and humans. As a human himself, he represents other humans before God, especially in his task of offering sacrifices for sins. Secondly (5:2-3), the high priest stands in solidarity with other humans because he shares their weakness. Thus he can show compassion to "the ignorant and erring." And as he offers the atoning sacrifices, he does so both for his own sins and for the sins of others. Thirdly (5:4), the high priest is called by God as Aaron was (see Exod 28:1) and does not take up the office on his own. More important than Aaronic/levitical descent for establishing Jesus' right to priesthood are the criteria of mediatorship, solidarity with others, and divine appointment. According to these criteria, it is possible to call Jesus our "great high priest."

The author applies these criteria in reverse order. The divine appointment of Christ as high priest is established in 5:5-6 by means of quotations from the author's favorite biblical passages—Psalms 2 and 110. The author assumes that the speaker is God and the one addressed is Christ. Both psalms were used in coronation rituals for kings in ancient Israel, and so can be called "messianic." Since for the author and other early Christians the key to the Scriptures is Christ, these two oracles are understood to concern Christ. The first oracle (Ps 2:7 = Heb 5:5) establishes that Christ is God's Son (see Heb 1:5), and the second oracle (Ps 110:4 = Heb 5:6) introduces the idea (to be developed at great length in Hebrews 7) of the eternal priesthood of Christ "according to the order of Melchizedek." The two quotations interpreted from a christological perspective are put forward as proof that God has called and appointed Christ to be the great high priest.

Christ's solidarity with other humans is established in 5:7-8 by reference to his suffering—a universal human experience: "he learned obedience from what he suffered." The description of Christ's suffering most vividly evokes the episode in Gethsemane (see Mark 14:32-42; Matt 26:36-46; Luke 22:39-46) but probably also encompasses all of his passion and death and indeed his entire life "in the flesh." The reference to his "prayers and supplications with loud cries and tears" places Jesus in the context of the many Old Testament lament psalms (see Psalms 3, 5, etc., and especially Psalm 22). From the author's christological perspective on biblical interpretation, Christ has become the speaker par excellence of the lament psalms. And in his case, "because of his reverence," his prayers were heard, and he was vindicated through his resurrection and exaltation.

Christ's mediatorship, according to 5:9-10, surpasses that of any other priest: "when he was made perfect, he became the source of eternal salvation for all who obey him." The reference to Christ's being made perfect alludes to his having reached his "goal" through his death and resurrection, which in turn has made possible "eternal salvation for all who obey him." No other priest could bring about eternal salvation. The best that the Old Testament priests could do was the annual Day of Atonement ritual with its hope that the people's sins of the past year would be wiped away. The final verse (5:10) anticipates the full treatment of the different priesthood of Christ "according to the order of Melchizedek" in chapter 7.

EXPLORING LESSON TWO

1. According to Hebrews, in what ways is Christ greater than Moses (3:1-6)?

2. Hebrews calls on its audience to persevere in faith "until the end," (3:14), a call echoed elsewhere in Scripture (see Matt 24:13; Luke 21:19; Acts 14:22; Rom 2:7; Jas 1:2-4). Have there been periods in your life when you found it difficult to persevere in your faith? How did you overcome such challenges and remain faithful to the Lord?

3. History can be a powerful tool for shaping our lives and decisions. What in salvation history does the author of Hebrews use as a warning to his audience (3:7-19)?

4. a) What are the multiple meanings of "rest" as used by the author of Hebrews (see 3:11, 18; 4:1-11)?

b) What does "rest" mean for you? How do you strive to keep the Sabbath (Sunday for Christians) as a day of rest?

5. To what does the term "today" refer in Hebrews (3:7, 13, 15; 4:7)?

6. a) Does the metaphor of a "two-edged sword" as a description of God's word resonate with you (4:12)? Why or why not?

b) In what ways have you experienced the "sharpness" of God's word? Has reading Scripture ever revealed things about yourself that you hadn't realized before?

7. Nothing is concealed from God, and to God we must "render an account" of our actions at the end of our lives (4:13). At the same time, in Christ we have a judge who is able to "sympathize with our weaknesses" (4:15-16). In what ways do you find comfort in the vision of judgement described here?

8. How do you understand the author's assertion that Jesus "learned obedience from what he suffered" (5:8)?

9. What does Hebrews mean when it says that Jesus was "made perfect" (5:9)?

10. What aspect of Jesus' suffering do you find most fruitful for reflection (his suffering in the garden of Gethsemane, his passion or death, or other aspects of his life)?

CLOSING PRAYER

Prayer

Indeed, the word of God is living and effective, sharper than any two-edged sword, penetrating even between soul and spirit, joints and marrow, and able to discern reflections and thoughts of the heart.

(Heb 4:12)

Merciful Father, with perfect knowledge you see all our deeds and discern all our thoughts. Sustain us by your holy word. May our hearts be pierced by its wisdom and our lives moved to compassion through its inspiration. Today we pray especially for . . .

LESSON THREE

Hebrews 5:11–7:28

Begin your personal study and group discussion with a simple and sincere prayer such as:

Prayer

Lord Jesus, by your death, resurrection, and exaltation, you have freed us from our sins. May our study of Hebrews increase our gratitude for this gift of salvation and inspire in us a desire to share with others your saving love.

Read the Bible text of Hebrews 5:11–7:28 found in the outside columns of pages 40–46, highlighting what stands out to you.

Read the accompanying commentary to add to your understanding.

Respond to the questions on pages 47–49, Exploring Lesson Three.

The Closing Prayer on page 50 is for your personal use and may be used at the end of group discussion.

IV: Jesus' Eternal Priesthood and Eternal Sacrifice

Exhortation to Spiritual Renewal

[11]About this we have much to say, and it is difficult to explain, for you have become sluggish in
hearing. [12]Although you should be teachers by this time, you need to have someone teach you again the basic elements of the utterances of God.
You need milk, [and] not solid food. [13]Everyone
who lives on milk lacks experience of the word of
righteousness, for he is a child. [14]But solid food is
for the mature, for those whose faculties are trained by practice to discern good and evil.

CHAPTER 6

[1]Therefore, let us leave behind the basic teaching about Christ and advance to maturity, without laying the foundation all over again: repentance from
dead works and faith in God, [2]instruction about
baptisms and laying on of hands, resurrection of
the dead and eternal judgment. [3]And we shall do
this, if only God permits. [4]For it is impossible in

continue

5:11–6:12 A call to Christian maturity

Hebrews is not simply a theological treatise. It is a sermon that interweaves biblical exposition and theology with reflections on the spiritual condition of the audience. Between his discussions of Christ's high priesthood in 4:14–5:10 and 7:1-28, the author issues a call to spiritual maturity (5:11–6:12) and offers an assurance about God's promises (6:13-20).

The call to Christian maturity in 5:11–6:12 consists of a reprimand (5:11–6:3), a stern warning (6:4-8), and a word of hope and encouragement (6:9-12). In the first part of the reprimand (5:11-14) the author admits that his topic of Christ's priesthood is "difficult to explain." But he locates the difficulty not so much in the material but rather in the audience ("you have become sluggish in hearing"). He goes on in 5:12 to scold them for failing to advance in Christian life. By this time they should have become teachers but in fact they stand in need of learning again the basic elements (the ABCs) of Christian faith. They remain in Christian infancy: "You need milk, [and] not solid food." In 5:13-14 he develops the contrast between the spiritually immature as lacking "experience of the word of righteousness" and the spiritually mature who can "discern good and evil." The Christian ideal is the integration of doctrine and practice.

The second part of the reprimand (6:1-3) challenges the congregation to move forward in their theological education and practice. The author urges them not to remain at the basic level, without of course neglecting the basics entirely—no more than one can neglect one's ABCs in writing or reading. The list of basics in 6:1b-2 is founded on "repentance from dead works and faith in God." Initiation into Christian life is covered by "baptisms and laying on of hands," while life-after-death is treated in "resurrection of the dead and eternal judgment." As they became Christians, the members of the congregation learned the distinctively Christian interpretations of Jewish beliefs and practices. Even though they seemed to be wavering about these matters, the author hopes

the case of those who have once been enlightened
and tasted the heavenly gift and shared in the holy
Spirit 5and tasted the good word of God and the
powers of the age to come, 6and then have fallen
away, to bring them to repentance again, since they
are recrucifying the Son of God for themselves and
holding him up to contempt. 7Ground that has
absorbed the rain falling upon it repeatedly and
brings forth crops useful to those for whom it is
cultivated receives a blessing from God. 8But if it
produces thorns and thistles, it is rejected; it will
soon be cursed and finally burned.

9But we are sure in your regard, beloved, of
better things related to salvation, even though we
speak in this way. 10For God is not unjust so as to
overlook your work and the love you have dem-
onstrated for his name by having served and con-
tinuing to serve the holy ones. 11We earnestly
desire each of you to demonstrate the same eager-
ness for the fulfillment of hope until the end, 12so
that you may not become sluggish, but imitators
of those who, through faith and patience, are in-
heriting the promises.

continue

that by moving them forward to "advanced" teaching about Christ's priesthood and sacrifice all these issues will fall into place again for them. As a good preacher, however, he acknowledges in 6:3 that their progress depends ultimately on God ("if only God permits").

The stern warning in 6:4-8 (see 10:26-31) is intended to shock the community into recognizing the seriousness of turning aside from Christian faith. The author declares that repentance after apostasy is impossible for those who have been "enlightened and tasted the heavenly gift and shared in the holy Spirit"—a general description of Christian initiation (which need not be broken down into the separate sacraments of baptism, Eucharist, and confirmation)—and "tasted the good word of God and the powers of the age to come"—a reference to God's word encountered in the Old Testament and in the preached gospel and to the signs and wonders that were part of early Christian experience. Those who fall away from Christian faith are said to be recrucifying the Son of God and holding him up to contempt. The theology of this stern warning seems to be that since Christ's death has made possible the forgiveness of sins, those who reject its saving significance have nowhere else to go for repentance and forgiveness. The rhetorical force of the warning seeks to awaken the community to recognize the seriousness of their situation.

The stark choice that is before the community is illustrated in 6:7-8 by the contrast between the good soil and the bad soil (see Mark 4:3-9; Matt 13:3-9; Luke 8:4-8). Whereas the good soil that produces useful crops receives a blessing from God (see Gen 1:11-12), the bad soil that produces only thorns and thistles is cursed (see Gen 3:17-18) and burned off. This dramatic contrast underscores how serious a decision lay before the wavering Christians. Will they produce good fruits and be blessed by God in Christ? Or will they produce thorns and thistles, and so share in the curse imposed upon Adam?

Having gotten the congregation's attention by his stern warning, the preacher in 6:9-12 offers some mitigating words of hope and encouragement. He first expresses in 6:9-10 confidence that his dear friends will enjoy the "better things related to salvation" because God will surely recognize their good works and the love that they have shown in serving their fellow Christians ("the holy ones"). Then in 6:11-12 he expresses his personal solicitude ("we earnestly desire") that they will persevere and so come to the fullness of what they can hope for in Christ. The stern warning of 6:4-8 has been replaced by the soothing talk of 6:9-12. But as the final comments in 6:12 indicate, the problem of spiritual sluggishness remains. If they are to enjoy what God has promised, they need to imitate the faith and patience shown by their spiritual forebears—a theme developed at length in Hebrews 11.

God's Promise Immutable

[13]When God made the promise to Abraham,
since he had no one greater by whom to swear, "he
swore by himself," [14]and said, "I will indeed bless you
and multiply" you. [15]And so, after patient waiting,
he obtained the promise. [16]Human beings swear by
someone greater than themselves; for them an oath
serves as a guarantee and puts an end to all argu-
ment. [17]So when God wanted to give the heirs of his
promise an even clearer demonstration of the im-
mutability of his purpose, he intervened with an
oath, [18]so that by two immutable things, in which it
was impossible for God to lie, we who have taken
refuge might be strongly encouraged to hold fast to
the hope that lies before us. [19]This we have as an
anchor of the soul, sure and firm, which reaches into
the interior behind the veil, [20]where Jesus has entered
on our behalf as forerunner, becoming high priest
forever according to the order of Melchizedek.

continue

The **symbolism of an anchor** in Hebrews 6:19 is unique in Scripture. There is no word in biblical Hebrew for "anchor" and, when the term is used elsewhere in the New Testament (as in Acts 27), no symbolic meaning is at play. The symbolic use of an anchor in ancient Greek literature as an emblem of stability is widespread. As an image of steadfast hope in Christianity, the anchor has a long history. Drawings of "anchor crosses" have been found in the Roman catacombs, and the anchor has continued to be part of Christian iconography down to the present day.

6:13-20 An assurance about God's promises

The reference to "inheriting the promises" in 6:12 provides the occasion for an assurance about God's promises in 6:13-20, which in turn prepares for the reflection in 7:1-28 about God's promise of a priest "according to the order of Melchizedek" in Psalm 110:4.

The key biblical text in the assurance is Genesis 22:16-17, in which God, impressed by Abraham's willingness to sacrifice his son Isaac, promises to Abraham many descendants. The two key points in the text for the author of Hebrews according to 6:13-15 are the content of the promise and the oath formula by which it is introduced ("he swore by himself"). The content of the promise is " 'I will indeed bless you and multiply' you." The oath formula is distinctive precisely because God "swore by himself." And the result is that Abraham obtained the promise "after patient waiting"—mostly likely not through Isaac alone but superabundantly through Christ.

In 6:16-18 the preacher continues his reflection on the oath and the promise of Genesis 22:16-17. In 6:16 he sets forth two basic principles of law: We humans customarily swear an oath by someone greater ("so help me God"), and we use an oath to end an argument ("I swear to God"). Then in 6:17-18 he refers back to Genesis 22:16-17 to make the case that God's promise is based not only on the content of the promise itself but also on the oath that precedes it. We can trust God's promise to Abraham and his descendants (in Christ) because it is based on "two immutable things"—God's word and God's oath. The significance of these reflections will become clearer in the meditation on Psalm 110:4 in chapter 7.

The final two verses (6:19-20) bring the listeners back to the topic of the high priesthood of Christ, which will be treated at length in chapter 7. They also introduce two striking images. God's promise fulfilled in Christ is "an anchor of the soul" (6:19), and Jesus is the "forerunner"—the leader who has gone before us to eternal life with God (6:20). As the high priest of Leviticus 16 entered the Holy of Holies on the Day of Atonement, so Christ has gone before us to enter God's heavenly court.

7:1-28 Jesus as a priest according to the order of Melchizedek

After moving from the first reflection on Christ's priesthood in 4:14–5:10 to exhortation in 5:11–6:20, the author returns to his main theological topic: Jesus' priesthood according to the order of Melchizedek.

In the Old Testament Melchizedek appears only in Genesis 14:17-20 and Psalm 110:4. These two passages will serve as the biblical basis for the author's argument about the superiority and eternal character of the priesthood of Christ. Although there were some speculations about Melchizedek in early Jewish and Christian writings, here the author is concerned only with establishing his points on the basis of these two biblical texts. How he handles them reveals much about Jewish biblical interpretation in the first century A.D. and about the Christian conviction that Christ is the key to the Scriptures.

CHAPTER 7

Melchizedek, a Type of Christ

1This "Melchizedek, king of Salem and priest of
God Most High," "met Abraham as he returned
from his defeat of the kings" and "blessed him."
2And Abraham apportioned to him "a tenth of ev-
erything." His name first means righteous king, and
he was also "king of Salem," that is, king of peace.
3Without father, mother, or ancestry, without be-
ginning of days or end of life, thus made to resemble
the Son of God, he remains a priest forever.

4See how great he is to whom the patriarch
"Abraham [indeed] gave a tenth" of his spoils.
5The descendants of Levi who receive the office
of priesthood have a commandment according to
the law to exact tithes from the people, that is,
from their brothers, although they also have come
from the loins of Abraham. 6But he who was not
of their ancestry received tithes from Abraham
and blessed him who had received the promises.
7Unquestionably, a lesser person is blessed by a

continue

Who Was Melchizedek?

The mysterious nature of Melchizedek and his enigmatic appearance in the Old Testament (Gen 14:17-20; Ps 110:4) have inspired numerous attempts at interpretation over the centuries, many of which are contradictory. For example, while most commentators who have understood "Salem" as a geographical place have associated it with Jerusalem, St. Jerome argued that the correct identification was likely Salim, a city in the upper Jordan valley where John baptized (John 3:23). Some modern scholars have suggested still other possible locations for the seat of Melchizedek's kingdom, including Shechem and Shiloh.

The person of Melchizedek himself has likewise been a source of widely divergent conjecture. More than one church father identified Melchizedek as Shem, son of Noah. A more radical and apparently widespread belief in the fourth century was that Melchizedek was actually God the Father, a heretical opinion that Epiphanius of Salamis (A.D. 315–403) wrote an entire treatise to refute.

As for references to Melchizedek outside of Scripture, fragmentary scrolls recovered at Qumran assign him an eschatological function, making him a deliverer of divine judgement in some undesignated future year of jubilee (11QMelch). Similarly, in the Babylonian Talmud, Melchizedek is named as one of the "four workmen" (Zech 2:3) who will defeat the enemies of Israel at the time of the Messiah (*Sukkah* 52b).

greater. [8]In the one case, mortal men receive
tithes; in the other, a man of whom it is testified
that he lives on. [9]One might even say that Levi
himself, who receives tithes, was tithed through
Abraham, [10]for he was still in his father's loins
when Melchizedek met him.
[11]If, then, perfection came through the levitical
priesthood, on the basis of which the people re-
ceived the law, what need would there still have
been for another priest to arise according to the
order of Melchizedek, and not reckoned accord-
ing to the order of Aaron? [12]When there is a
change of priesthood, there is necessarily a change
of law as well. [13]Now he of whom these things are
said belonged to a different tribe, of which no
member ever officiated at the altar. [14]It is clear that
our Lord arose from Judah, and in regard to that
tribe Moses said nothing about priests. [15]It is even
more obvious if another priest is raised up after
the likeness of Melchizedek, [16]who has become
so, not by a law expressed in a commandment
concerning physical descent but by the power of
a life that cannot be destroyed. [17]For it is testified:

continue

Hebrews is the sole book in the New Testament to refer to Jesus as a **"high priest."** In Jewish tradition the high priest was the main cultic figure and leader of the Sanhedrin, the chief legal body in Judaism at the time of Jesus. Although this position was sometimes inherited, it also became a politically important position at the time when Rome ruled the Holy Land. The origins of the high priesthood are obscure, most likely originating in the postexilic period of Israel's history.

The reflection on Genesis 14:17-20 in Hebrews 7:1-10 seeks to show the superiority of Christ's priesthood to the Jewish levitical priesthood. In 7:1-2a the author introduces Melchizedek as "king of Salem and priest of God Most High" and focuses on the two matters of greatest importance to his argument: Melchizedek blessed Abraham as he returned from battle, and Abraham gave to Melchizedek a tithe or "tenth of everything."

In 7:2b-3 the author considers the person of Melchizedek. His name can be interpreted in Hebrew to mean "king of righteousness" or "righteous king." Likewise, the name of his city "Salem" (which was most likely Jerusalem) can be associated with the Hebrew word for "peace." As righteous king and king of peace, Melchizedek was a type of Christ. Moreover, in Genesis 14:17-20 Melchizedek comes out of nowhere. He is given no genealogy ("without father, mother, or ancestry"), and nothing is said about his birth or death ("without beginning of days or end of life"). Scripture's silence about Melchizedek's origins and fate contributes to the author's case that Melchizedek prefigures the eternal Son of God. But the real focus of attention is the superior priesthood of Melchizedek and Christ.

The rest of the argument on the basis of Genesis 14:17-20 in 7:4-10 focuses on the acts of blessing and tithing. By Jewish custom the superior figure blesses the inferior figure. By Jewish custom all the other tribes pay a tithe or tax to support the priestly tribe of Levi (see Num 18:21-24). But according to Genesis 14:17-20 Abraham gave a tenth of all his spoils (a tithe) to Melchizedek, who had blessed Abraham. Both actions show the superiority of Melchizedek to Abraham. Since the patriarch Levi—from whom the Jewish levitical priests traced their lineage—was a descendant of Abraham, these two actions, according to the reasoning of the author of Hebrews, suggest the anteriority and superiority of Melchizedek's priesthood to that of Levi. It is as if Levi, before he was born, had already acknowledged the superiority of Melchizedek and so of Christ. The next step in the argument is to prove that Christ's priesthood is the priesthood of Melchizedek.

The reflection on Psalm 110:4 in Hebrews 7:11-28 seeks to establish the eternal character of Christ's priesthood. The text is quoted in

> "You are a priest forever
> according to the order of Melchizedek."
>
> [18]On the one hand, a former commandment is
> annulled because of its weakness and uselessness,
> [19]for the law brought nothing to perfection; on
> the other hand, a better hope is introduced,
> through which we draw near to God. [20]And to
> the degree that this happened not without the
> taking of an oath—for others became priests
> without an oath, [21]but he with an oath, through
> the one who said to him:
>
> "The Lord has sworn, and he will not repent:
> 'You are a priest forever'"—
>
> [22]to that same degree has Jesus [also] become the
> guarantee of an [even] better covenant. [23]Those
> priests were many because they were prevented by
> death from remaining in office, [24]but he, because
> he remains forever, has a priesthood that does not
> pass away. [25]Therefore, he is always able to save
> those who approach God through him, since he
> lives forever to make intercession for them.
>
> [26]It was fitting that we should have such a high
> priest: holy, innocent, undefiled, separated from
> sinners, higher than the heavens. [27]He has no
> need, as did the high priests, to offer sacrifice day
> after day, first for his own sins and then for those
> of the people; he did that once for all when he
> offered himself. [28]For the law appoints men sub-
> ject to weakness to be high priests, but the word
> of the oath, which was taken after the law, ap-
> points a son, who has been made perfect forever.

7:17: "You are a priest forever / according to the order of Melchizedek." The oracle is introduced by an oath formula, which is quoted in 7:21: "The Lord has sworn, and he will not repent: / 'You are a priest . . .'" The author contends that the promise (ratified by an oath) of an eternal priesthood in Psalm 110:4 has been fulfilled in Christ.

Having established the anteriority and superiority of Melchizedek's priesthood in 7:1-10, the author now argues that the priesthood of Melchizedek has found its fulfillment in Christ, and that Christ's priesthood has superseded that of Levi. Whereas the events described in Gen 14:17-20 preceded chronologically the law of Moses and the levitical priesthood, the oracle in Psalm 110:4 (whose origin in David's time is assumed) came later than the law of Moses and the levitical priesthood.

In 7:11 the author reasons that if the levitical priesthood brought "perfection" (see 7:28), there would have been no need for God to promise another priesthood in Psalm 110:4. He observes in 7:12 that a change of priesthood implies a change of law. This is part of his argument that Christ represents better promises and a better covenant.

There was, however, an obvious obstacle to calling Jesus a priest in a Jewish context. Jesus did not belong to the priestly tribe of Levi. Rather, he belonged to the royal tribe of Judah through King David. The author freely admits this fact in 7:13-14. How then could Jesus be called a priest? This was made possible through Jesus' resurrection from the dead. Jesus became a priest "by the power of a life that cannot be destroyed" (7:16), thus fulfilling the promise of an eternal priesthood ("forever") in Psalm 110:4. His priesthood replaced the weak and imperfect priesthood of Levi. Because Christ's priesthood has provided an access to God that was impossible under the old priesthood, it has introduced "a better hope" (7:18-19), which is eternal life with God.

The eternal priesthood of Christ is based according to 7:20-22 not only on the promise of God ("You are a priest forever") but also on the oath of God ("The Lord has sworn, and he will not repent"). At this point the author builds on his reflections about two immutable things—God's promise and God's oath—in 6:13-20. Just as Christ's priesthood means "a change of law" (7:12) and "a better hope" (7:19), so it is also "the guarantee of an [even] better covenant" (7:22). The levitical priesthood was not eternal, since the levitical priests died (7:23). But since the risen Christ lives forever, his priesthood is eternal (7:24), and so he is "always" able to make intercession with God (which is what priests do) for "those who approach God through him" (7:25).

Multiple sacrifices were offered each day in the Jerusalem temple and included not only the communal morning and evening sacrifices prescribed in Exodus 29:38-42, but also the many sacrifices offered by individuals for various reasons. Once a year, on the Day of Atonement, the high priest offered sacrifice for his and all the people's sins. In Hebrews 7:27, the author appears to have conflated all of these sacrifices together when he refers to the high priest offering "sacrifice day after day, first for his own sins and then for those of the people."

The concluding reflection in 7:26-28 highlights the heavenly character of Christ's priesthood. He is "holy, innocent, undefiled, separated from sinners, higher than the heavens" (7:26). His death on the cross represents the one, perfect sacrifice. And so he has no need to offer sacrifices every day for his own sins and the sins of others. In describing the perfect sacrifice of Christ in 7:27 the author summarizes the theology of his entire work: "he did that once for all when he offered himself." Christ is both the priest (the one who offers sacrifice) and the victim (what is offered), and his sacrifice has value "once for all." There is no need for other sacrifices or other priests in the light of Jesus' one, perfect sacrifice.

The final verse (7:28) argues for the superiority and eternal character of Christ's priesthood on three counts. Whereas the law merely "appoints" high priests, the oracle about Christ's priesthood in Psalm 110:4 is accompanied by a divine oath. Whereas the levitical high priests were subject to "weakness," the risen Christ is the Son of God "made perfect forever." Whereas the levitical priesthood was part of the law of Moses, Christ's priesthood, which came later than the law not only with regard to Christ but also to Psalm 110:4, is the key to the better covenant—the primary topic of chapter 8.

EXPLORING LESSON THREE

1. St. Ignatius of Loyola described a state of "desolation" as finding ourselves apathetic, tepid, and sad. Hebrews warns its audience against becoming "sluggish in hearing" (5:11). When you feel you are slipping into a state of lukewarmness, how do you revitalize your faith life?

2. a) What was your reaction to the likening of apostates, or those who have fallen away from the faith, to those who would "recrucify" the Son of God and hold him up to contempt (6:6)?

   b) Why did the author of Hebrews so sternly condemn apostasy?

3. Who are the "holy ones" mentioned in Hebrews 6:10? Do you find anything surprising about this designation?

4. What two "immutable things" (6:18) give us assurance that God will keep his promises?

5. In what way does Melchizedek resemble the Son of God (7:2b-3)?

6. How do the tithes Abraham gave to Melchizedek and the blessing given to him in return demonstrate that Melchizedek's priesthood was greater than the levitical priesthood established by the Mosaic law (7:4-10)?

7. According to Hebrews, how could Jesus, who did not belong to the priestly tribe of Levi, be called a priest (7:13-16)?

8. How does the author of Hebrews use Psalm 110 to establish the eternal character of Christ's priesthood (7:11-28)?

9. In what way can the sacrifice offered by Jesus be considered more effective than those offered by the priests of the old covenant?

10. a) How does the depiction of Jesus in Hebrews 7:26 contrast with that in Hebrews 4:15-16?

    b) Which of these depictions resonates with you more? Why?

CLOSING PRAYER

Prayer

Therefore, he is always able to save those who approach God through him, since he lives forever to make intercession for them.

(Heb 7:25)

Eternal and merciful Lord Jesus, you are the gate through which sinners pass with confidence to draw near the Father. While we live, keep us firm in faith and practice, so that one day we may receive the gift of salvation won for us by your sacrifice on the cross. We offer this prayer for ourselves and for all, especially . . .

LESSON FOUR

Hebrews 8:1–10:18

Begin your personal study and group discussion with a simple and sincere prayer such as:

Prayer

Lord Jesus, by your death, resurrection, and exaltation, you have freed us from our sins. May our study of Hebrews increase our gratitude for this gift of salvation and inspire in us a desire to share with others your saving love.

Read the Bible text of Hebrews 8:1–10:18 found in the outside columns of pages 52–59, highlighting what stands out to you.

Read the accompanying commentary to add to your understanding.

Respond to the questions on pages 60–62, Exploring Lesson Four.

The Closing Prayer on page 63 is for your personal use and may be used at the end of group discussion.

CHAPTER 8

Heavenly Priesthood of Jesus

[1]The main point of what has been said is this: we have such a high priest, who has taken his seat at the right hand of the throne of the Majesty in heaven, [2]a minister of the sanctuary and of the true tabernacle that the Lord, not man, set up. [3]Now every high priest is appointed to offer gifts and sacrifices; thus the necessity for this one also to have something to offer. [4]If then he were on earth, he would not be a priest, since there are those who offer gifts according to the law. [5]They worship in a copy and shadow of the heavenly sanctuary, as Moses was warned when he was about to erect the tabernacle. For he says, "See that you make everything according to the pattern shown you on the mountain." [6]Now he has obtained so much more excellent a ministry as he is mediator of a better covenant, enacted on better promises.

continue

8:1-6 Jesus' heavenly priesthood

Having established the eternal character of Christ's priesthood on the basis of Psalm 110:4, the author argues that the place of Christ's priesthood and sacrifice is heaven. As a good preacher, he offers in 8:1 both a recapitulation ("we have such a [great] high priest") and a transition to the next topic (heaven as the locus of Christ's priestly ministry). Here Psalm 110:1 ("The LORD says to my lord: / 'Sit at my right hand . . .'"), which was already cited in 1:13 (see also 1:3), serves as one starting point. The other starting point is the early Christian belief that Jesus, having really died, was raised from the dead and now lives with God in glory ("at the right hand of the throne of the Majesty in heaven").

The two main topics of 8:2-5 are the sanctuary and the sacrifices associated with Christ's priesthood. The sanctuary where Christ ministers has been established by God, not by human beings. It is therefore the "true tabernacle" in the sense that every earthly sanctuary is a copy and shadow of the heavenly sanctuary. This theme is developed in 8:5.

Before that, however, the author must treat in 8:3-4 the heavenly nature of Christ's sacrifices. If Christ were on earth, he would not be offering sacrifices since by the definition of the law of Moses he would not be a priest (because he was from the tribe of Judah, not of Levi). But of course, the sacrifice of Christ was his own self in his death on the cross. Those priests who function on earth do so at an earthly sanctuary and offer earthly gifts and sacrifices to God. Their sanctuary is only "a copy and shadow of the heavenly sanctuary" (8:5).

Such language is reminiscent of Plato's teaching that the visible world is but a copy and shadow of the ideal world. A more likely source, however, is God's instruction to Moses in Exodus 25:40 when Moses began to construct the tabernacle: "See that you make everything according to the pattern shown you on the mountain." The idea is that God gave Moses a "blueprint" or prototype of the tabernacle on Mount Sinai. The heavenly sanctuary of Christ's priesthood is "the real thing," and other sanctuaries are at best poor imitations. Since the author had already established the "better promises" and the "more excellent" character of Christ's ministry, 8:6

functions as another summary. It also serves as a transition, since it introduces the theme of a "better covenant."

The idea that the earthly tabernacle was but a "shadow of the **heavenly sanctuary**" (8:5) was prevalent among the Israelites, not only in reference to the tabernacle constructed by Moses but to the Jerusalem temple as well. The concept of a "heavenly sanctuary" was further elaborated in non-biblical Jewish works such as *The Testament of Levi*, which describes archangels acting as ministers in a heavenly sanctuary, where continual offerings are made to the Lord "for the sins of ignorance of the righteous" (*T. Levi* 3:5).

8:7-13 The old and new covenants

This section contains the longest continuous Old Testament quotation in the New Testament. The text is the prophecy of God's new covenant with his people that appears in Jeremiah 31:31-34. The historical background is the prophet's recognition that soon Jerusalem and its temple would be captured and destroyed by the Babylonians in the early sixth century B.C. While often described as a prophet of doom, Jeremiah was also a prophet of hope. His hope was based on God's fidelity to his people and to his promises,

Old and New Covenants

7For if that first covenant had been faultless, no place would have been sought for a second one. 8But he finds fault with them and says:

"Behold, the days are coming, says the Lord,
when I will conclude a new covenant with the house of Israel and the house of Judah.
9It will not be like the covenant I made with their fathers
the day I took them by the hand to lead them forth from the land of Egypt;
for they did not stand by my covenant
and I ignored them, says the Lord.
10But this is the covenant I will establish with the house of Israel
after those days, says the Lord:
I will put my laws in their minds
and I will write them upon their hearts.
I will be their God,
and they shall be my people.
11And they shall not teach, each one his fellow citizen
and kinsman, saying, 'Know the Lord,'
for all shall know me,
from least to greatest.
12For I will forgive their evildoing
and remember their sins no more."

continue

The Old and New Covenants

Hebrews explicitly contrasts the new and old covenants. The author finds the old covenant inferior in every way, when compared to the new covenant established in Jesus Christ and predicted in Jeremiah (Jer 31:31-34). One must be cautious, however, not to conclude that the first covenant no longer has value. Indeed, the *Catechism of the Catholic Church* is clear that "the Old Covenant has never been revoked" (*CCC* 121; see also Rom 9:4). Vatican Council II noted: "The apostle Paul maintains that the Jews remain very dear to God, for the sake of the patriarchs, since God does not take back the gifts he bestowed or the choice he made" (*NA* 4). For this reason, although the church sees the old covenant as a preparation for the new, God continues to relate to the Jewish people as a chosen people called always into faithfulness to the God whose love for them has never ceased and whose covenant with them remains in effect.

[13]When he speaks of a "new" covenant, he declares the first one obsolete. And what has become obsolete and has grown old is close to disappearing.

CHAPTER 9

The Worship of the First Covenant

[1]Now [even] the first covenant had regulations for worship and an earthly sanctuary. [2]For a tabernacle was constructed, the outer one, in which

continue

not on the strength of Judah's armies and kings. His prophecy of a new covenant looks forward to a restored and superior relationship between God and Israel, one more perfect than anything that Israel had yet experienced.

The author in 8:7 introduces the quotation by observing that if the first covenant had been perfect and without blemish, there would have been no need for a second or new covenant. At this point, and in 8:13, his only explicit interest is with the word "new" in the promise of a new covenant. Nevertheless, there are other themes in Jeremiah 31:31-34 that are also important, especially the ideas of God's renewed relationship with Israel, the internal appropriation of the new covenant ("in their minds . . . upon their hearts"), and the forgiveness of sins.

The concluding comment in 8:13 explores the implications of the "new" covenant. Such language, according to the author, makes the first covenant "obsolete." He goes on to qualify that strong term by explaining that "what has become obsolete and has grown old is close to disappearing." That was the perspective of the prophet Jeremiah, for he recognized the catastrophe that would soon fall upon Judah in the early sixth century B.C. Is it also the perspective of the author of Hebrews? If so, to what does he refer? Could it be the Jerusalem temple (which was destroyed in A.D. 70), the institutions of the Old Testament (priesthood, sanctuary, sacrifices, etc.), or Judaism in general?

9:1-10 The earthly sanctuary

Having argued that the sanctuary of Christ's priesthood is in heaven, the author explains that the earthly sanctuary described in Exodus 25–26 was a shadow or "parable" of the real thing. He also prepares for the characterization of Christ's perfect sacrifice in 9:11–10:18 in terms of the rituals of the Day of Atonement (Leviticus 16).

The "earthly sanctuary" of the first covenant is described in 9:1-5 in terms of its "regulations" (which in 9:10 are called "regulations concerning the flesh"). Taking his information from Exodus 25–26, the author first in 9:2 mentions the outer tent or tabernacle, with its furnishings consisting of the lampstand, the table, and the bread of offering. The name of the outer tent is "the Holy Place." The inner tent is called "the Holy of Holies," the place where only the high priest could enter once a year on the Day of Atonement (9:3-5). Its furnishings—the gold altar of incense, the gilded ark of the covenant, a gold jar containing manna, Aaron's staff, and the tablets of God's covenant with Moses—are more exotic and elaborate than those of the Holy Place. The list is drawn from the book of Exodus and from popular traditions, not necessarily from the realities of the Second Temple. The most important feature of the inner tent, however, is "the place of expiation" (often translated as "the mercy seat"), the place in the Holy of Holies that was sprinkled with blood by the high priest on the Day of Atonement (see Lev 16:14-15; Rom 3:25). Recognizing that prolonging these descriptions might lead to distraction, the author in 9:5 abruptly breaks off his treatment ("now is not the time . . .").

To highlight further the importance of the rituals of the Day of Atonement, the preacher in 9:6-7 contrasts what happened in the outer tent and what happened in the inner tent. Whereas in the Holy Place many priests repeatedly performed their sacrifices for sins, only the high priest might enter the Holy of Holies once a year for the purpose of sprinkling blood there "for himself and for the sins of the people."

The Old Testament does not explicitly state that any object was contained in the **ark of the covenant** other than the tablets on which the Ten Commandments were written (Exod 25:16). According to Scripture, both the jar of manna (Exod 16:32-34) and Aaron's staff (Num 17:16-26) were to be placed "in front of" the ark of the covenant in the tabernacle's inner sanctuary. It is likely that the close proximity of the ark and the other two objects eventually led to the belief that they were placed inside it.

Reproduction of ark of the covenant.

were the lampstand, the table, and the bread of
offering; this is called the Holy Place. 3Behind the
second veil was the tabernacle called the Holy of
Holies, 4in which were the gold altar of incense
and the ark of the covenant entirely covered with
gold. In it were the gold jar containing the manna,
the staff of Aaron that had sprouted, and the tab-
lets of the covenant. 5Above it were the cherubim
of glory overshadowing the place of expiation.
Now is not the time to speak of these in detail.
6With these arrangements for worship, the
priests, in performing their service, go into the
outer tabernacle repeatedly, 7but the high priest
alone goes into the inner one once a year, not
without blood that he offers for himself and for
the sins of the people. 8In this way the holy Spirit
shows that the way into the sanctuary had not yet
been revealed while the outer tabernacle still had
its place. 9This is a symbol of the present time, in
which gifts and sacrifices are offered that cannot
perfect the worshiper in conscience 10but only in
matters of food and drink and various ritual wash-
ings: regulations concerning the flesh, imposed
until the time of the new order.

continue

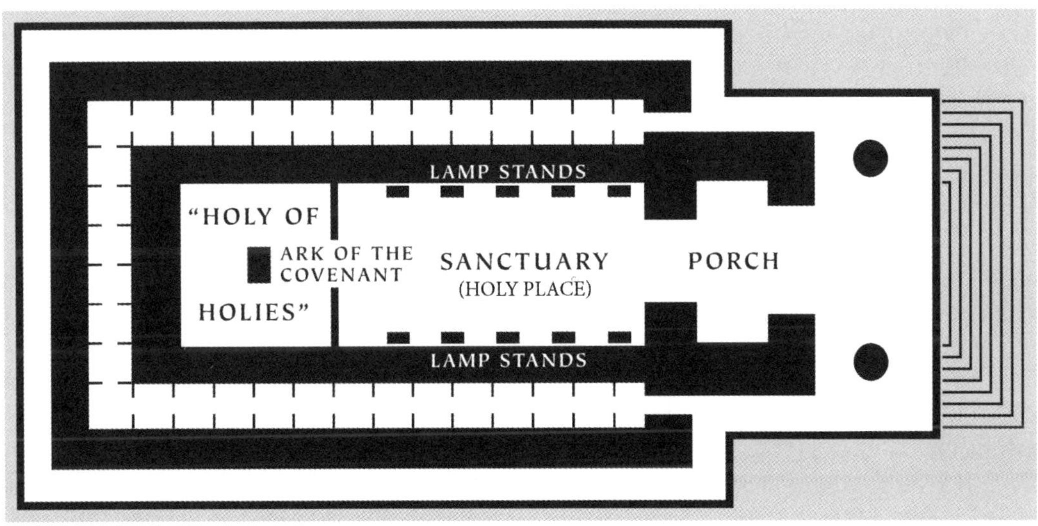

Diagram of the temple, which replaced the desert tabernacle.

Sacrifice of Jesus

[11]But when Christ came as high priest of the
good things that have come to be, passing through
the greater and more perfect tabernacle not made
by hands, that is, not belonging to this creation,
[12]he entered once for all into the sanctuary, not
with the blood of goats and calves but with his
own blood, thus obtaining eternal redemption.
[13]For if the blood of goats and bulls and the sprin-
kling of a heifer's ashes can sanctify those who are
defiled so that their flesh is cleansed, [14]how much
more will the blood of Christ, who through the
eternal spirit offered himself unblemished to
God, cleanse our consciences from dead works to
worship the living God.
[15]For this reason he is mediator of a new cove-
nant: since a death has taken place for deliverance
from transgressions under the first covenant,
those who are called may receive the promised
eternal inheritance. [16]Now where there is a will,
the death of the testator must be established. [17]For

continue

The "place of expiation" (9:5), often referred to as the **mercy seat**, was understood to be the lid or covering of the ark of the covenant itself (see Exod 25:17; 37:6). Since it was on this covering that blood was sprinkled on the Day of Atonement for the sins of the people, some scholars note the possible dual meaning of the Hebrew word for "cover" (*kapporet*), since it may refer to both the physical lid for the ark and the "covering" or atonement for sins that was the purpose of the annual ritual.

However important the rituals of the Day of Atonement might seem, they were inadequate when compared with the perfect sacrifice of Christ (9:8-10). These institutions of the old covenant were used by the holy Spirit to foreshadow the genuine "way into the sanctuary" that Christ the high priest would reveal (9:8). They belonged to "the present time" and could not perfect persons in the depth of their being ("in conscience"). They were "regulations concerning the flesh" that were in force "until the time of the new order" or "the age to come" that has been inaugurated by Christ's life, death, resurrection, and exaltation. They functioned as symbols or parables, dealt with earthly things (food, drink, ablutions, etc.), were open to only a select few (the priests), and were imperfect by nature. They pointed to the perfect sacrifice of Christ offered in his death on the cross for us and for our sins.

9:11-28 The efficacy of Christ's blood

The essence of the Day of Atonement ritual was the high priest's sprinkling of animal blood inside the Holy of Holies. Based on the idea of blood as a symbol of life and as an agent of purification, this action was believed to take away the past sins of the people (including those of the high priest himself) and to prepare them for renewed life before God in the new year. For the author of Hebrews, Christ is both the perfect high priest and the perfect sacrifice (in his death on the cross). His blood, shed only once, accomplished what the blood of animals shed annually could not achieve.

In 9:11-14 the author affirms that Christ the "high priest of the good things that have come to be" ("the age to come," which is already here) has entered the divinely constructed tent (heaven) with his own blood (not animal blood) as the perfect sacrifice offered once for all, with "eternal redemption" as its result. He celebrates the greater efficacy of Christ's sacrifice by arguing in 9:13-14 with the rhetorical technique of "from the lesser to the greater." If the animal blood used in earthly sacrifices had any efficacy with regard to the body, how much more has Christ's perfect sacrifice on the cross ("the blood of Christ") cleansed consciences from sins and made it possible to worship the living God. By entering the heavenly sanctuary with his blood, Christ provided an effective cleansing from sin and made possible right relationship with God (what Paul calls "justification").

In 9:15-22 the author contends that the blood of Christ has inaugurated the new covenant prophesied by Jeremiah. Christ is the mediator of that new covenant through his death on the cross (9:15). To explain this point in 9:16-17, he plays on the double meaning of "testament," which can refer to a "covenant" and to a "last will and testament." Just as a last will is activated only when the person dies, so the promise of the new covenant has been activated through the death of Christ. The result is redemption from sins under the old covenant and participation in the eternal inheritance. Just as the old covenant given to Moses on Sinai was ratified by the sprinkling of blood upon an altar (see Exod 24:3-8), so the new covenant has been ratified by the shedding of Christ's blood on the cross. In 9:22 the author describes blood as a means of purification and of forgiveness, and observes that "without the shedding of blood there is no forgiveness" (see Lev 17:11).

a will takes effect only at death; it has no force
while the testator is alive. [18]Thus not even the first
covenant was inaugurated without blood. [19]When
every commandment had been proclaimed by
Moses to all the people according to the law, he
took the blood of calves [and goats], together
with water and crimson wool and hyssop, and
sprinkled both the book itself and all the people,
[20]saying, "This is 'the blood of the covenant which
God has enjoined upon you.'" [21]In the same way,
he sprinkled also the tabernacle and all the vessels
of worship with blood. [22]According to the law
almost everything is purified by blood, and without the shedding of blood there is no forgiveness.
[23]Therefore, it was necessary for the copies of
the heavenly things to be purified by these rites,
but the heavenly things themselves by better sacrifices than these. [24]For Christ did not enter into
a sanctuary made by hands, a copy of the true one,
but heaven itself, that he might now appear before
God on our behalf. [25]Not that he might offer himself repeatedly, as the high priest enters each year
into the sanctuary with blood that is not his own;
[26]if that were so, he would have had to suffer repeatedly from the foundation of the world. But
now once for all he has appeared at the end of the
ages to take away sin by his sacrifice. [27]Just as it is
appointed that human beings die once, and after
this the judgment, [28]so also Christ, offered once
to take away the sins of many, will appear a second
time, not to take away sin but to bring salvation
to those who eagerly await him.

continue

Animals were sacrificed for the expiation of different offenses, many of which were not punishable by death according to Mosaic law. Sacrificial animals should not, therefore, be seen as *substitutes* for penitents. The real purpose of animal sacrifice was to release the animal's blood, which was recognized as its animating force. The **nature of blood**, seen as a symbol of the divine gift of life, made it the most effective means of purification from sin and reconciling God with humanity.

In 9:23-28 the author argues that by approaching God in the heavenly sanctuary with his own blood Christ brought about a complete purification of sins. But Christ's work is not simply a past event ("once for all," see 9:12). Rather, Christ the high priest continues to exercise a priestly ministry in heaven: "that he might now appear before God on our behalf" (9:24). Moreover, Christ the high priest will exercise a priestly ministry at the last judgment when he "will appear a second time" (9:28). Since he has already taken away sins by his death on the cross, then his task will be "to bring salvation to those who eagerly await him." Thus there are three phases in the priestly work of Christ: cleansing from sin (past), ongoing mediation on our behalf (present), and final deliverance (future).

CHAPTER 10

One Sacrifice instead of Many

1Since the law has only a shadow of the good
things to come, and not the very image of them, it
can never make perfect those who come to worship
by the same sacrifices that they offer continually
each year. 2Otherwise, would not the sacrifices have
ceased to be offered, since the worshipers, once
cleansed, would no longer have had any conscious-
ness of sins? 3But in those sacrifices there is only a
yearly remembrance of sins, 4for it is impossible that
the blood of bulls and goats take away sins. 5For this
reason, when he came into the world, he said:

"Sacrifice and offering you did not desire,
but a body you prepared for me;
6holocausts and sin offerings you took no
delight in.
7Then I said, 'As is written of me in the scroll,
Behold, I come to do your will, O God.'"

8First he says, "Sacrifices and offerings, holocausts
and sin offerings, you neither desired nor de-
lighted in." These are offered according to the law.

continue

10:1-18 Christ as the effective priest and sacrifice

As he reaches the close of his reflections on the priesthood and sacrifice of Christ, the author in 10:1-4 insists that the repeated sacrifices under the law of Moses were ineffective. At best they were "a shadow of the good things to come" as opposed to the true form or image, and so they were incapable of making perfect those who offered them at the Day of Atonement (10:1). The very fact that these sacrifices were repeated every year shows their inability to bring about real atonement for sins (10:2-3). Finally the author asserts in 10:4 that the blood of bulls and goats cannot take away sins.

Next in 10:5-10 the author contends that the many sacrifices offered according to the law of Moses have been superseded by the one perfect sacrifice of Christ. To make this point he places the words of Psalm 40:5-7 in the mouth of Christ "when he came into the world" (the incarnation) as a statement of Christ's vocation and the superiority of his sacrifice. In 10:8 the author identifies the sacrifices of Psalm 40 with those offered according to the law of Moses. Then in 10:9-10 he goes on to contrast those sacrifices with the one perfect sacrifice of Christ's body offered on the cross. His sacrifice has superseded and even abolished the animal sacrifices. Only the one perfect sacrifice of Jesus Christ was able to make people holy ("consecrated"). That sacrifice was offered in a spirit of faithful obedience to God's will: "Behold, I come to do your will."

Just as the many sacrifices under the law have been superseded by the one sacrifice of

Christ, so according to 10:11-14 the many priests have been replaced by the one priest. Under the law of Moses there were many priests who offered the same sacrifices over and over without being able to take away sins (10:11). However, Christ the one great high priest "offered one sacrifice for sins" (in his death on the cross) and has been exalted to God's right hand (Jesus' resurrection and ascension, described in terms of Ps 110:1). The one perfect sacrifice of Christ is summarized as follows: "For by one offering he has made perfect forever those who are being consecrated."

Whereas the repeated sacrifices by the priests of the old covenant were ineffective, the one sacrifice of Christ the priest of the new covenant brings about the forgiveness of sins. The motif of the new covenant is introduced by quotations from Jeremiah 31:31-34 in 10:15-17. The new covenant that is inscribed on hearts and minds matches the total interior obedience of Christ ("I come to do your will"). The new covenant wipes away sins and allows God's people to make a new start. So effective is the one perfect sacrifice of Christ in forgiving sins that there is no need for any more sacrifices: "Where there is forgiveness of these, there is no longer offering for sin" (10:18). Thus the sacrificial system of the old covenant, which was at best a "shadow" of Christ's sacrifice, has been superseded. From now on the forgiveness of sins is necessarily linked to Jesus' sacrificial death for us and for our sins. Other sacrifices have been rendered unnecessary.

9 Then he says, "Behold, I come to do your will."
He takes away the first to establish the second. 10 By
this "will," we have been consecrated through the
offering of the body of Jesus Christ once for all.

11 Every priest stands daily at his ministry, of-
fering frequently those same sacrifices that can
never take away sins. 12 But this one offered one
sacrifice for sins, and took his seat forever at the
right hand of God; 13 now he waits until his ene-
mies are made his footstool. 14 For by one offering
he has made perfect forever those who are being
consecrated. 15 The holy Spirit also testifies to us,
for after saying:

> 16 "This is the covenant I will establish with
> them after those days, says the Lord:
> 'I will put my laws in their hearts,
> and I will write them upon their minds,'"

17 he also says:

> "Their sins and their evildoing
> I will remember no more."

18 Where there is forgiveness of these, there is no
longer offering for sin.

EXPLORING LESSON FOUR

1. a) What is the relationship between the earthly sanctuary built by Moses and the "true tabernacle" where the everlasting ministry of Christ is enacted (8:1-6)?

   b) What events or experiences in your life might you identify as a "copy" or "shadow" of a later, more substantial experience?

2. In what way does Jeremiah 31:31-34 support the idea that a new covenant between God and Israel would one day be needed (8:7-13)?

3. What are some possible interpretations of the statement that the first covenant between God and Israel "has become obsolete and has grown old [and] is close to disappearing" (8:13)?

4. a) In the earthly sanctuary, what is the most important feature of the "Holy of Holies" (9:1-5)?

b) What differentiates the sacrifices that were performed by the priests in the outer tabernacle from the sacrifice performed by the high priest in the Holy of Holies on the Day of Atonement (9:6-7)?

5. What is the essential ingredient common to the sacrifices performed in the old covenant and that performed by Christ (9:11-28)? What is different about Christ's sacrifice?

6. Christ's second coming is described here in the context of judgement (9:27-28), a theme found throughout Hebrews (6:2, 8; 4:13; 10:26-31). Do you find such references to divine judgment reassuring or frightening?

7. Chronologically speaking, what are the three phases in the priestly ministry of Christ (9:23-28)?

8. Read Matthew 9:13 and 12:7, two places where Jesus quotes Hosea 6:6. How is Jesus' assertion similar to Hebrews in regard to animal sacrifice (10:1-10)?

9. How can believers internalize the law of the new covenant as described in Hebrews 10:16? What is the result of this inner transformation?

10. As a follower of Jesus Christ, how have you experienced the power of Christ's sacrifice on the cross in your own life?

CLOSING PRAYER

Prayer

"Then I said, 'As is written of me in the scroll,
Behold, I come to do your will, O God.'"
(Heb 10:7)

Merciful Savior, you are the mirror of deep humility and perfect obedience. Grant us the grace to imitate you more and more each day. May we always prefer God's will to our own, desiring only to serve you, and to serve one another in your love. Today we pray especially for . . .

LESSON FIVE

Hebrews 10:19–11:40

Begin your personal study and group discussion with a simple and sincere prayer such as:

Prayer

Lord Jesus, by your death, resurrection, and exaltation, you have freed us from our sins. May our study of Hebrews increase our gratitude for this gift of salvation and inspire in us a desire to share with others your saving love.

Read the Bible text of Hebrews 10:19–11:40 found in the outside columns of pages 66–71, highlighting what stands out to you.

Read the accompanying commentary to add to your understanding.

Respond to the questions on pages 72–74, Exploring Lesson Five.

The Closing Prayer on page 75 is for your personal use and may be used at the end of group discussion.

Recalling the Past

19Therefore, brothers, since through the blood
of Jesus we have confidence of entrance into the
sanctuary 20by the new and living way he opened
for us through the veil, that is, his flesh, 21and since
we have "a great priest over the house of God," 22let
us approach with a sincere heart and in absolute
trust, with our hearts sprinkled clean from an evil
conscience and our bodies washed in pure water.
23Let us hold unwaveringly to our confession that
gives us hope, for he who made the promise is
trustworthy. 24We must consider how to rouse one
another to love and good works. 25We should not
stay away from our assembly, as is the custom of
some, but encourage one another, and this all the
more as you see the day drawing near.
26If we sin deliberately after receiving knowledge
of the truth, there no longer remains sacrifice for
sins 27but a fearful prospect of judgment and a flam-
ing fire that is going to consume the adversaries.
28Anyone who rejects the law of Moses is put to
death without pity on the testimony of two or three
witnesses. 29Do you not think that a much worse
punishment is due the one who has contempt for
the Son of God, considers unclean the covenant-
blood by which he was consecrated, and insults the
spirit of grace? 30We know the one who said:

"Vengeance is mine; I will repay,"

and again:

"The Lord will judge his people."

continue

PERSEVERANCE IN CHRISTIAN LIFE

Heb 10:19–13:25

10:19-39 A call to persevere in faith

Following a pattern set in 5:11–6:12, this passage consists of an appeal (10:19-25), a stern warning (10:26-31), and a word of encouragement (10:32-39). It ends on a note of faith, which prepares for the catalogue of the heroes of faith in chapter 11.

Using language reminiscent of 4:14-16, the author in 10:19-21 provides a theological foundation for his appeal by affirmations about what has happened through Jesus' death, resurrection, and exaltation. Through the blood of Christ we have access to the heavenly sanctuary and have a great high priest who mediates with God on our behalf. The three appeals in 10:22-25 feature the virtues of faith, hope, and love. The call to approach God in faith ("with a sincere heart and in absolute trust") in 10:22 builds upon the conviction that Christ's perfect sacrifice has brought about the forgiveness of sins—an experience that is symbolized in baptism. The call to persevere in Christian hope in 10:23 builds upon the trustworthiness of God and of God's promises. The call to live in love with fellow Christians in 10:24-25 builds upon the need for Christian community to be the place where Christians encourage one another to love and to do good works in preparation for the Day of the Lord (judgment). The passing observation that some were absenting themselves from the Christian assembly (10:25) is another symptom of the ecclesial situation of the community to which the author wrote.

The stern warning in 10:26-31 (see 6:4-8) again concerns a post-baptismal sin of the most serious kind—apostasy (see 10:29). If one rejects Christ after having embraced Christian faith, there is no effective sacrifice for one's sins because the sacrifices of the old covenant have been superseded and the all-sufficient sacrifice of Christ has been rejected. All that remains for such persons is the "fearful prospect" of judgment and punishment. The seriousness of their sin is highlighted by another argument "from the lesser to the greater." If according to Deuteronomy 17:6 a person may be put to death for idolatry or blasphemy on the testimony of two or three human witnesses, how much greater will the punishment be for those who spurn the Son of God, profane the blood of God's covenant, and commit outrages against the holy Spirit. The fearsome character of God's judgment is reinforced by quotations from Deuteronomy 32:35-36: "Vengeance is mine; I will repay . . . The Lord will judge his people." This stern warning concludes with one of the most menacing sentences in Scripture: "It is a fearful thing to fall into the hands of the living God" (10:31).

As in 6:9-12, the stern warning is balanced by a word of hope and encouragement in 10:32-39. The author in 10:32-34 urges the community to recall what they suffered shortly after having become Christians ("after you had been enlightened"). The way in which

31 It is a fearful thing to fall into the hands of the
living God.
32 Remember the days past when, after you had
been enlightened, you endured a great contest of
suffering. 33 At times you were publicly exposed to
abuse and affliction; at other times you associated
yourselves with those so treated. 34 You even joined
in the sufferings of those in prison and joyfully
accepted the confiscation of your property, know-
ing that you had a better and lasting possession.
35 Therefore, do not throw away your confidence;
it will have great recompense. 36 You need endur-
ance to do the will of God and receive what he
has promised.

37 "For, after just a brief moment,
he who is to come shall come;
he shall not delay.
38 But my just one shall live by faith,
and if he draws back I take no pleasure
in him."

39 We are not among those who draw back and
perish, but among those who have faith and will
possess life.

continue

"Sinners in the Hands of an Angry God"

Jonathan Edwards' famous 1741 sermon (still read in many high school literature classes), "Sinners in the Hands of an Angry God," was not based on Hebrews 10:31 but Deuteronomy 32:35. Still, the Calvinist minister's message mirrors that found in Hebrews, as both texts contain stern warnings of divine judgment. While we may find the rhetoric in Edward's sermon excessive today ("God holds you over the pit of Hell, much as one holds a spider or some loathsome insect over the fire"), the real difference between his vision and that found in Hebrews is Edwards' failure to balance his concept of divine "vengeance" with the certainty of hope we have in Jesus, our compassionate high priest, who is able to "sympathize with our weaknesses," tested as we are "in every way, yet without sin" (4:15).

Rev. Jonathan Edwards

V: Examples, Discipline, Disobedience

CHAPTER 11

Faith of the Ancients

[1]Faith is the realization of what is hoped for and
evidence of things not seen. [2]Because of it the an-
cients were well attested. [3]By faith we understand
that the universe was ordered by the word of God,
so that what is visible came into being through the
invisible. [4]By faith Abel offered to God a sacrifice
greater than Cain's. Through this he was attested
to be righteous, God bearing witness to his gifts,
and through this, though dead, he still speaks. [5]By
faith Enoch was taken up so that he should not see
death, and "he was found no more because God
had taken him." Before he was taken up, he was
attested to have pleased God. [6]But without faith it
is impossible to please him, for anyone who ap-
proaches God must believe that he exists and that
he rewards those who seek him. [7]By faith Noah,
warned about what was not yet seen, with rever-
ence built an ark for the salvation of his household.
Through this he condemned the world and inher-
ited the righteousness that comes through faith.

[8]By faith Abraham obeyed when he was called
to go out to a place that he was to receive as an
inheritance; he went out, not knowing where he

continue

these sufferings are described—public abuse, imprisonment, and confiscation of property—may reflect conditions that prevailed in Rome for some Christians in the late fifties or early sixties of the first century A.D. The preacher's point is that the new Christians endured these sufferings joyfully because they were convinced that they had "a better and lasting possession" (10:34). He goes on in 10:35-36 to exhort these people to confidence and endurance in the present situation out of the conviction that they will surely be rewarded by God ("great recompense . . . receive what he has promised"). Then in 10:37-38 he appeals to the second coming of Christ with a christological interpretation of Isaiah 26:20 ("he who is to come shall come") and urges perseverance in faith by quoting Habakkuk 2:4 ("my just one shall live by faith"). He ends in 10:39 by counting himself and his community "among those who have faith and will possess life," thus preparing for the catalogue of biblical exemplars of faith in chapter 11.

Many attempts have been made to identify the **"great contest of suffering"** (10:32) endured by Hebrews' original audience. Some possibilities that have been suggested include: the early persecution of the Jerusalem church (Acts 8:1); the expulsion of Jewish Christians from Rome in A.D. 49 by Claudius; the Roman persecution under Nero in A.D. 64; and the civil and social persecution of Jewish Christians following the first Jewish-Roman war in A.D. 66–73.

11:1-40 Examples of persevering faith

To explain what it means to be "among those who have faith and will possess life" (10:39), the author presents a catalogue of figures from the Old Testament who provide models of persevering faith in God's promises. Similar lists of biblical heroes can be found in Sirach 44–49 and Wisdom 10:1–11:4. What distinguishes the list in Hebrews 11 is the resolute emphasis on "by faith." For the author of Hebrews, faith involves the knowledge of unseen realities, a generous response to God's call, a hopeful trust in God's promises, and faithful endurance in the face of suffering and death.

What may appear to be an abstract definition of faith in 11:1-2 is more a programmatic statement to be illustrated by the examples that follow. That faith involves trust in God's promises ("what is hoped for . . . things not seen") is clear. The problem comes with the Greek words *hypostasis* ("realization") and *elenchos* ("evidence"), and whether they are to be taken as objectively as those translations suggest or in a more subjective way ("assurance . . . conviction"). Of course, faith involves both objective and subjective dimensions, as the following examples will show.

The first examples (11:3-7) correspond to events and figures in Genesis 1–11. The work of creation described in Genesis 1 (see Heb 11:3) was carried out by the power of God's word, and we understand this to be so "by faith." The reason why God accepted the sacrifice of Abel rather than that of Cain (see Gen 4:1-7) is attributed in 11:4 to Abel's superior faith and righteousness. The reason why Enoch was taken up into heaven (see Gen 5:24) was his great faith, according to 11:5. The case of Enoch leads to a brief reflection in 11:6 on the life of faith as the only life that is pleasing to God and on the necessity for belief in God and in God's desire to reward those who seek him. In the cases of creation, Abel's sacrifice, and Enoch's assumption, the author has provided an interpretation ("by faith") that is not explicit in the biblical texts. In the case of Noah (Heb 11:7) he has a strong biblical example of faith. According to Genesis 6:8-22, Noah obeyed God's command to build an ark on the strength of his trust in God's promises "about what was not yet seen" and he was rewarded by "the salvation of his household." Noah's act of faith was both a witness against the corrupt world and a foreshadowing of Abraham's "righteousness that comes through faith."

was to go. 9By faith he sojourned in the promised
land as in a foreign country, dwelling in tents with
Isaac and Jacob, heirs of the same promise; 10for
he was looking forward to the city with foundations, whose architect and maker is God. 11By
faith he received power to generate, even though
he was past the normal age—and Sarah herself
was sterile—for he thought that the one who had
made the promise was trustworthy. 12So it was
that there came forth from one man, himself as
good as dead, descendants as numerous as the
stars in the sky and as countless as the sands on
the seashore.

13All these died in faith. They did not receive
what had been promised but saw it and greeted
it from afar and acknowledged themselves to be
strangers and aliens on earth, 14for those who
speak thus show that they are seeking a homeland.
15If they had been thinking of the land from
which they had come, they would have had opportunity to return. 16But now they desire a better
homeland, a heavenly one. Therefore, God is not
ashamed to be called their God, for he has prepared a city for them.

17By faith Abraham, when put to the test, offered up Isaac, and he who had received the promises was ready to offer his only son, 18of whom it

continue

Interestingly, the story of **Cain and Abel** in Genesis 4:1-16 is ambiguous about why Abel's sacrifice was "greater" than Cain's (Heb 11:4). Philo of Alexandria devoted an entire treatise to considering this question, and the problem was subsequently taken up by many of the church fathers, including St. Ambrose and St. Augustine.

A second set of biblical examples of faith is provided by Abraham and other patriarchs in 11:8-22. According to 11:8-10, faith is what motivated Abraham to leave his homeland and to enter the promised land of Canaan (see Gen 12:1-4), even though he did not know where he was going. And yet by "dwelling in tents" he acknowledged that the promised land of Canaan was not to be his perfect and final abode. Rather, it was a sign or shadow of the heavenly city of God, "the city with foundations, whose architect and maker is God." Faith, according to 11:11-12, is what enabled Abraham and Sarah to accept the promise (see Gen 17:15-22) that despite their advanced ages and her sterility they would have a son named Isaac, and that their descendants would be as many as "the stars in the sky" and "the sands was said, "Through Isaac descendants shall bear your name." [19]He reasoned that God was able to raise even from the dead, and he received Isaac back as a symbol. [20]By faith regarding things still to come Isaac blessed Jacob and Esau. [21]By faith Jacob, when dying, blessed each of the sons of Joseph and "bowed in worship, leaning on the top of his staff." [22]By faith Joseph, near the end of his life, spoke of the Exodus of the Israelites and gave instructions about his bones.

[23]By faith Moses was hidden by his parents for three months after his birth, because they saw that he was a beautiful child, and they were not afraid of the king's edict. [24]By faith Moses, when he had grown up, refused to be known as the son of Pharaoh's daughter; [25]he chose to be ill-treated along with the people of God rather than enjoy the fleeting pleasure of sin. [26]He considered the reproach of the Anointed greater wealth than the treasures of Egypt, for he was looking to the recompense. [27]By faith he left Egypt, not fearing the king's fury, for he persevered as if seeing the one who is invisible. [28]By faith he kept the Passover and sprinkled the blood, that the Destroyer of the firstborn might not touch them. [29]By faith they crossed the Red Sea as if it were dry land, but when the Egyptians attempted it they were drowned. [30]By faith the walls of Jericho fell after being encircled for seven days. [31]By faith Rahab the harlot did not perish with the disobedient, for she had received the spies in peace.

continue

on the seashore." Abraham's faith rested on the person of God: "for he thought that the one who had made the promise was trustworthy" (Heb 11:11).

In 11:13-16 the author interrupts his list for a reflection on the as-yet-unfulfilled or eschatological nature of the faith displayed by Abraham and Sarah and indeed by all the great Old Testament exemplars of faith. Since "all these died in faith," they failed to enjoy during their lifetimes on earth the fullness of life with God—something that has been made possible through Jesus' death, resurrection, and exaltation. Rather, they remained "strangers and aliens on earth" (11:14; see Gen 23:4) in search of a homeland. However, they recognized that their true homeland was not the land from which they came (and to which they could return) but rather the city that God had prepared for them in heaven. What these heroes of faith hoped for has become a reality through Christ.

The theme of the as-yet-unfulfilled character of the patriarchs' faith is developed by further examples in 11:17-22. Faith moved Abraham to offer his son Isaac as a sacrifice to God, despite the fact that God's promise of many descendants was to be through Isaac (Heb 11:17-19). What made Abraham willing to obey God's command was, according to the author, a belief in God's power to raise the dead back to life, and so Isaac was a symbol foreshadowing the resurrection of Jesus. The blessings bestowed by Isaac and Jacob (11:20-21) were signs of their hopes for future generations. The observation that Jacob gave his blessing while "leaning on the top of his staff" (see Gen 47:31 in the Greek version) adds to the "pilgrim" motif of faith. The fact that Joseph gave instructions about the Exodus from Egypt and about moving his bones out of Egypt (11:22; see Gen 50:24-25) indicates the incomplete nature of what he experienced and his trust that there would be much more to the promises of God.

The faith displayed by the patriarchs was also at work in Moses and in the Exodus generation according to 11:23-31. Faith led Moses' parents to conceal him in defiance of Pharaoh's decree to kill the male infants of the Hebrews (11:23; see Exod 2:1-10). Faith led Moses to identify himself not with the royal household of Egypt but rather with Israel as the people of God (11:24-27; see Exod 2:11-15), even though this meant suffering "the reproach of the Anointed" and so prefiguring the sufferings of Christ. Faith led Moses to command the elders of Israel in Egypt to sprinkle blood from the Passover lambs at the doors of the residences of the Hebrews (11:28; see Exod 12:21-23). He had no guarantee beyond his faith in God's promises that this action would protect the Israelites from "the Destroyer of the firstborn." Faith led Moses and others to cross the Red Sea with the conviction that they would emerge safely and that the Egyptians would not do so (11:29; see Exod 14:22-28). Faith led Joshua to trust that the walls of Jericho would fall (11:30; see Josh 6:12-21), and faith led the Gentile prostitute Rahab to ally herself with the people of God by protecting the Israelite spies (11:31; see Josh 2:1-21; 6:22-25).

Several of the **unnamed examples of faith** mentioned in Hebrews 11:32-38 can be identified with some degree of confidence. Daniel is likely the one who "closed the mouths of lions," while his fellow Israelites Shadrach, Meshach, and Abednego (who survived the fiery furnace of Nebuchadnezzar) may be those who "put out raging fires" (Dan 3:46-50; 6:21-23). The reference to those who "were tortured and would not accept deliverance, in order to obtain a better resurrection" recalls the seven brothers and their mother who willingly suffered torture and death rather than violate God's law in 2 Maccabees 7. Zechariah the prophet was stoned to death (2 Chron 24:21), while, according to legend, Isaiah was sawn in half with a wooden saw.

32What more shall I say? I have not time to tell
of Gideon, Barak, Samson, Jephthah, of David and
Samuel and the prophets, 33who by faith conquered
kingdoms, did what was righteous, obtained the
promises; they closed the mouths of lions, 34put
out raging fires, escaped the devouring sword; out
of weakness they were made powerful, became
strong in battle, and turned back foreign invaders.
35Women received back their dead through resur-
rection. Some were tortured and would not accept
deliverance, in order to obtain a better resurrection.
36Others endured mockery, scourging, even chains
and imprisonment. 37They were stoned, sawed in
two, put to death at sword's point; they went about
in skins of sheep or goats, needy, afflicted, tor-
mented. 38The world was not worthy of them. They
wandered about in deserts and on mountains, in
caves and in crevices in the earth.

39Yet all these, though approved because of their
faith, did not receive what had been promised.
40God had foreseen something better for us, so that
without us they should not be made perfect.

A good preacher knows when to bring a topic to its conclusion ("What more shall I say?"), and so in 11:32-38 he summarizes the subsequent history of God's people. After a list of heroes (11:32), he gives examples of triumphant faith in 11:33-35a and still more examples of endurance in the face of suffering in 11:35b-38. These heroes bore their sufferings out of faith in the resurrection (see 11:35a), which was appropriate since this world "was not worthy of them" (11:38a).

However great was the faith that these heroes displayed, they nonetheless did not yet receive what had been promised (11:39-40). What God promised was forgiveness of sins and eternal life with God—something made possible through Jesus' death, resurrection, and exaltation.

We all have **role models**—people who inspire us and provide us with a pattern of life to imitate. We also look to role models for our spiritual lives. While saints who are formally recognized by the church can be spiritual exemplars for us, there may also be people we know personally—family members, friends, fellow parishioners, coworkers—whose faith-filled lives are worthy of imitation. Who is your spiritual role model?

EXPLORING LESSON FIVE

1. a) How have our hearts been "sprinkled clean from an evil conscience" (10:22)? (See also Heb 9:13-14.)

   b) What might the reference to "washing" refer to (10:22)? (See also Heb 6:2.)

2. Hebrews 10:24 speaks of the need for Christians to "rouse one another to love and good works." How have you encouraged friends and/or family members to live their faith in action? Who has encouraged you in this way?

3. Unlike Hebrews' original audience, most of us have not "endured a great contest of suffering" for our faith (10:32), and yet this text still holds relevance for us today. What struggles have you faced as a result of your faith? How does the message of Hebrews encourage or inform you in those struggles?

4. a) What distinguishes the catalogue of biblical heroes found in Hebrews 11 from similar lists found in Sirach 44–49 and Wisdom 10:1–11:4?

b) How does the author of Hebrews understand "faith" as it is presented here in Hebrews 11?

5. According to Genesis 6:11, Noah lived at a time when "the earth was corrupt in the view of God and full of lawlessness," and yet he persevered in his faith in God (11:7, 13-16). In what way can we draw inspiration from Noah's perseverance in his faith?

6. What does the fact that Abraham continued to dwell in tents after his arrival in Canaan indicate (11:9)?

7. In what way could Isaac be seen as a symbol foreshadowing the resurrection of Jesus (11:17-19)?

8. Which of the biblical exemplars of faith mentioned in Hebrews 11 do you find the most inspiring or interesting, and why?

9. The fact that many of the Old Testament figures who serve as examples of enduring faith in Hebrews 11 did not live to see the fulfillment of what they hoped for makes their faith all the more remarkable. How have their hopes become reality through Christ?

CLOSING PRAYER

Prayer

You need endurance to do the will of God and receive what he has promised. (Heb 10:36)

Holy Spirit, there is so much in our lives that saps our spiritual strength and weakens our resolve to love and serve you. Send us the grace to persevere in faith, hope, and love. We pray today especially for . . .

LESSON SIX

Hebrews 12–13

Begin your personal study and group discussion with a simple and sincere prayer such as:

Prayer

Lord Jesus, by your death, resurrection, and exaltation, you have freed us from our sins. May our study of Hebrews increase our gratitude for this gift of salvation and inspire in us a desire to share with others your saving love.

Read the Bible text of Hebrews 12–13 found in the outside columns of pages 78–84, highlighting what stands out to you.

Read the accompanying commentary to add to your understanding.

Respond to the questions on pages 85–87, Exploring Lesson Six.

The Closing Prayer on page 88 is for your personal use and may be used at the end of group discussion.

CHAPTER 12

God Our Father

[1]Therefore, since we are surrounded by so great
a cloud of witnesses, let us rid ourselves of every
burden and sin that clings to us and persevere in
running the race that lies before us [2]while keeping
our eyes fixed on Jesus, the leader and perfecter
of faith. For the sake of the joy that lay before him
he endured the cross, despising its shame, and has
taken his seat at the right of the throne of God.
[3]Consider how he endured such opposition from
sinners, in order that you may not grow weary and
lose heart. [4]In your struggle against sin you have
not yet resisted to the point of shedding blood.
[5]You have also forgotten the exhortation ad-
dressed to you as sons:

"My son, do not disdain the discipline of
the Lord
or lose heart when reproved by him;
[6]for whom the Lord loves, he disciplines;
he scourges every son he acknowledges."

[7]Endure your trials as "discipline"; God treats you
as sons. For what "son" is there whom his father

continue

The use of **athletic imagery** to describe the Christian life (12:1-2) is common in the New Testament, especially in the letters of Paul (1 Cor 9:24; 1 Tim 6:12; 2 Tim 4:7). While Paul may envisage the goal of the race to be Jesus himself (Phil 3:14), St. John Chrysostom took a novel approach in his interpretation of Hebrews 12:1-2 by suggesting that we should keep "our eyes fixed on Jesus" in the same way that an athlete looks toward a coach, receiving instruction even while engaged in the race.

12:1-17 A call to persevere in faith

The heroes of faith celebrated in chapter 11 constitute a "cloud of witnesses" for Christians (12:1). Nevertheless, the Christians addressed in this sermon are still engaged in a struggle or race that demands endurance and discipline. In this contest they have the good example of Jesus as "the leader and perfecter of faith" (12:2). What is especially significant for them is Jesus' own willingness to endure the suffering and shame of the cross in full expectation of his exaltation to God's throne (see Ps 110:1) and the perfect joy of life in heavenly glory. For Jesus, the cross was a trial to be endured in the hope of glory.

In 12:3-4 the preacher addresses the community's own situation in the light of Christ's example. His endurance of hostility from sinners should inspire them to "not grow weary and lose heart" (12:3). Moreover, their situation, however serious it may seem, in fact has not yet reached the point of "shedding blood" (12:4), which suggests that they have not yet faced martyrdom.

To help the community to understand its present sufferings and to encourage them to persevere in faith, the author offers a reflection on the theme of suffering as a discipline, with Proverbs 3:11-12 as his main text. His emphasis is on the educative or formative (rather than punitive) value of suffering. In the biblical passage quoted in 12:5-6 the sage directs his student ("my son") to accept the divine discipline as a sign of God's love and concern for him. In the biblical world a father had the ultimate responsibility for child rearing (especially in the case of sons). In his first application in 12:7-8 the preacher suggests that their present sufferings are proof that God regards the Christians as legitimate "sons" for whom he takes responsibility.

He goes on in 12:9-11 to compare the discipline applied by earthly fathers with the discipline applied by God. If earthly fathers win respect from the sons whom they discipline, how much more should we respect "the Father of spirits" in our sufferings (12:9). Moreover, the benefits from divine discipline—sharing in God's holiness, and "the peaceful fruit of righteousness"—in the present and the future far outweigh the benefits that may come from a human father's application of discipline. Divine discipline is superior to human discipline in forming children of God.

Rather than obsessing over their present sufferings, the addressees need to get back on the "way" of discipleship. Using language from Isaiah 35:3 and Proverbs 4:26, the preacher in 12:12-13 urges them to pull themselves together and walk along the straight path with renewed spiritual energy. They also need to remove whatever hinders their spiritual progress. Therefore, according to 12:14, they need to strive for the peace and holiness that come from God and that bears witness to God in the world. They need to guard against the "bitter root" (see Deut 29:18) of division that can harm the life of the whole community (12:15). And they need to learn from the negative example of Esau, who because of his impatience and desire for momentary gratification (see Gen 25:29-34) sold his birthright to Jacob and could not get it back when he sought Isaac's blessing (see Gen 27:30-45). The case of Esau reiterates in a subtle way the author's previous stern warnings about the impossibility of repentance after apostasy (see 6:4-8 and 10:26-31).

does not discipline? 8If you are without discipline,
in which all have shared, you are not sons but
bastards. 9Besides this, we have had our earthly
fathers to discipline us, and we respected them.
Should we not [then] submit all the more to the
Father of spirits and live? 10They disciplined us
for a short time as seemed right to them, but he
does so for our benefit, in order that we may share
his holiness. 11At the time, all discipline seems a
cause not for joy but for pain, yet later it brings
the peaceful fruit of righteousness to those who
are trained by it.

12So strengthen your drooping hands and your
weak knees. 13Make straight paths for your feet,
that what is lame may not be dislocated but healed.

Penalties of Disobedience

14Strive for peace with everyone, and for that
holiness without which no one will see the Lord.
15See to it that no one be deprived of the grace of
God, that no bitter root spring up and cause
trouble, through which many may become defiled,
16that no one be an immoral or profane person like
Esau, who sold his birthright for a single meal.
17For you know that later, when he wanted to inherit his father's blessing, he was rejected because
he found no opportunity to change his mind, even
though he sought the blessing with tears.

continue

While there is nothing in Genesis that suggests Esau was either "immoral" or "profane" (12:16), later Jewish texts contain references to immorality in Esau's relationships with his Canaanite wives (e.g., Jubilees 25:1-8). The **negative view of Esau's character** later became even more pronounced in rabbinic literature where, for many writers like Philo of Alexandria, he came to represent the embodiment of human vice.

[18]You have not approached that which could be touched and a blazing fire and gloomy darkness and storm [19]and a trumpet blast and a voice speaking words such that those who heard begged that no message be further addressed to them, [20]for they could not bear to hear the command: "If even an animal touches the mountain, it shall be stoned." [21]Indeed, so fearful was the spectacle that Moses said, "I am terrified and trembling." [22]No, you have approached Mount Zion and the city of the living God, the heavenly Jerusalem, and countless angels in festal gathering, [23]and the assembly of the firstborn enrolled in heaven, and God the judge of all, and the spirits of the just made perfect, [24]and Jesus, the mediator of a new covenant, and the sprinkled blood that speaks more eloquently than that of Abel.

[25]See that you do not reject the one who speaks. For if they did not escape when they refused the one who warned them on earth, how much more in our case if we turn away from the one who warns from heaven. [26]His voice shook the earth at that time, but now he has promised, "I will once more shake not only earth but

continue

12:18-29 A call to heavenly worship

Through Christ's priestly sacrifice on the cross, we have access to God. What the institutions and rituals of the old covenant were powerless to do, Christ has accomplished by making possible right relationship with God (justification) and participation in the heavenly worship of God.

This point is developed in 12:18-24 by contrasting the old worship symbolized by Mount Sinai (12:18-21) and the new worship symbolized by Mount Zion (12:22-24). The description of Mount Sinai is taken mainly from Exodus 19 (see also Exod 20:18-21 and Deut 4:10), though what appears to be awesome in Exodus 19 is interpreted negatively as terrifying in Hebrews. The Sinai experience was full of violent images of storms, fire, and trumpet blasts. It featured a command (Exod 19:12-13) to stone any animal that touched the sacred mountain. Even Moses the mediator of the Sinai covenant confessed that he was "terrified and trembling" (Deut 9:19). By contrast, the new heavenly worship symbolized by Mount Zion is peaceful and joyful. Here Mount Zion is not the earthly city of Jerusalem but rather the heavenly Jerusalem (see Revelation 21–22), "the city of the living God." It is inhabited by angels, "the firstborn enrolled in heaven" (perhaps the saints of the Old Testament, Christian martyrs, or Christians who had already died), God the judge of all, and Jesus the mediator of a new covenant. Whereas Abel's blood bore witness against Cain's guilt and cried out for vengeance (see Gen 4:10), Jesus' blood spoke more eloquently in that it won forgiveness of sins and brought about perfect reconciliation with God.

There are several ways one might interpret the comparison between **Abel's blood and the blood of Christ** (12:24). Some commentators have suggested that, while both Abel and Christ shed blood as martyrs, the blood of Jesus has immeasurably greater salvific power. Other exegetes see the contrasting spatial terms, noting that Abel's blood remained on the earth (crying out to God "from the ground"; Gen 4:10) while Christ's blood, after his exaltation, was carried into the heavenly sanctuary where the Son still intercedes for us with the Father.

The contrast is followed by an admonition not to reject God's warning (12:25-29). In the new covenant of Mount Zion/heavenly Jerusalem it is God who speaks. If the people of the Sinai covenant refused to listen to Moses and were punished for their obduracy, how much more punishment can Christians expect if they fail to heed the heavenly voice of God and his Son (see 6:4-8; 10:26-31; 12:15-17).

While the author of Hebrews is generally concerned with realized eschatology (the present benefits of Christ's saving action) and spatial eschatology (heaven and earth), he does occasionally engage in temporal eschatology (as in 10:27-28). Here in 12:26-28 his biblical text is from Haggai 2:6: "I will once more shake not only earth but heaven." The earth shook at the giving of the old covenant at Mount Sinai (see Exod 19:18). But the sixth-century B.C. prophet Haggai spoke of a future shaking that would involve both earth and heaven. At God's future eschatological intervention both earth and heaven will shake. Nevertheless, the final shaking will be good news for those who have persevered in faith and in the worship of God. The result will be the removal of "shaken, created things" (12:27). Then the kingdom of God will be "the unshakable kingdom" in which the worship of God will be conducted "in reverence and awe." To those consoling and encouraging words, the preacher adds a concluding comment designed to bring his audience back to the serious challenge that faced them in the present: "For our God is a consuming fire" (12:29; see Deut 4:24; Isa 33:14).

Given Hebrews' frequent warnings against apostasy, the reference to God being a **"consuming fire"** (12:29) is particularly apt, since in its original context (Deut 4:24) the threat of arousing God's wrath is a consequence of abandoning the covenant. Fire is traditionally used in the Bible as a metaphor for God's judgment (Isa 33:14; Matt 25:41; 2 Pet 3:7), a theme that appears throughout Hebrews (6:2; 9:27; 10:27).

heaven." 27That phrase, "once more," points to
[the] removal of shaken, created things, so that
what is unshaken may remain. 28Therefore, we
who are receiving the unshakable kingdom should
have gratitude, with which we should offer wor-
ship pleasing to God in reverence and awe. 29For
our God is a consuming fire.

VI: Final Exhortation, Blessing, Greetings

CHAPTER 13

1Let mutual love continue. 2Do not neglect
hospitality, for through it some have unknowingly
entertained angels. 3Be mindful of prisoners as if
sharing their imprisonment, and of the ill-treated
as of yourselves, for you also are in the body. 4Let
marriage be honored among all and the marriage
bed be kept undefiled, for God will judge the im-
moral and adulterers. 5Let your life be free from
love of money but be content with what you have,
for he has said, "I will never forsake you or aban-
don you." 6Thus we may say with confidence:

"The Lord is my helper,
[and] I will not be afraid.
What can anyone do to me?"

continue

13:1-6 General instructions

Under the heading "let mutual love continue" (13:1), the author encourages the cultivation of the human virtues of hospitality, compassion, chastity, and avoidance of greed. In each case he provides a theological motivation.

As Acts and the New Testament epistles show, there was an extensive network of communication among early Christians. The virtue of hospitality toward emissaries (apostles) and other travelers was essential to its smooth functioning. The theological motive about receiving angels attached to the admonition not to neglect hospitality (13:2) alludes to episodes involving Abraham and Lot in Genesis 18 and 19. The directive to be mindful of prisoners and victims of torture (13:3) is accompanied by an appeal to human solidarity. The call to respect marriage and to avoid adultery (13:4) invokes God's judgment against fornicators and

7 Remember your leaders who spoke the word of
God to you. Consider the outcome of their way
of life and imitate their faith. 8 Jesus Christ is the
same yesterday, today, and forever.
9 Do not be carried away by all kinds of strange
teaching. It is good to have our hearts strength-
ened by grace and not by foods, which do not
benefit those who live by them. 10 We have an altar
from which those who serve the tabernacle have
no right to eat. 11 The bodies of the animals whose
blood the high priest brings into the sanctuary as
a sin offering are burned outside the camp.
12 Therefore, Jesus also suffered outside the gate,
to consecrate the people by his own blood. 13 Let
us then go to him outside the camp, bearing the
reproach that he bore. 14 For here we have no last-
ing city, but we seek the one that is to come.
15 Through him [then] let us continually offer God
a sacrifice of praise, that is, the fruit of lips that
confess his name. 16 Do not neglect to do good
and to share what you have; God is pleased by
sacrifices of that kind.
17 Obey your leaders and defer to them, for they
keep watch over you and will have to give an ac-
count, that they may fulfill their task with joy and
not with sorrow, for that would be of no advan-
tage to you.

continue

adulterers (see 1 Cor 5:13; Eph 5:5). The rejection of greed (13:5) is balanced by contentment with what God gives. The theological motive for such an attitude is trust in God as expressed in God's own promise according to Deuteronomy 31:6, 8. The concluding confession in 13:6 quotes Psalm 118:6 to the effect that confidence in God casts out all fear. In this short instruction the motives are quite varied: biblical precedents, human solidarity, divine judgment, and trust in God. The absence of a direct appeal to Christ in these instructions is unusual in a work that is as directly centered on Christ as Hebrews is.

13:7-17 Community life and worship

This section begins and ends with instructions about "leaders" (13:7-9 and 13:17), and contains an intervening reflection on worship (13:10-16). The leaders "who spoke the word of God to you" may include not only those who actually evangelized the group addressed in this work but also the apostles and even the Old Testament heroes of faith celebrated in chapter 11. The statement in 13:8 that "Jesus Christ is the same yesterday, today, and forever" sounds like an early Christian confession of faith, and at the same time fits well with the emphasis in Hebrews on Christ as the eternal leader of God's people. This confession is followed by a warning in 13:9 not to be swayed by "strange teaching." The example of "foods, which do not benefit those who live by them" may refer to the Old Testament sacrifices or to the Jewish food laws. If, however, Hebrews was directed to a Jewish Christian community at Rome (as many scholars think likely), then there may be an allusion to the struggle between the "weak" and the "strong" treated by Paul in Romans 14–15. The author of Hebrews clearly takes the side of the "strong."

The intervening section on worship (13:10-16) begins in 13:10 by making a distinction between the worship of the old covenant and the new covenant. The "altar" refers more likely to the heavenly sanctuary at which Christ the high priest presides than to a church building or even to community celebrations of the Eucharist. Those who continue to "serve the tabernacle" (under the old covenant) have no right to the "altar" of Christ (under the new covenant). If (as seems likely) the original addressees were Jewish Christians, this statement expresses a sharp distinction between "old covenant" Judaism and "new covenant" Jewish Christianity.

In 13:11-12 the author makes a final attempt to explain Jesus' death in terms of sacrifice. According to Leviticus 16:27, the carcasses of the animals whose blood was used in the Day of Atonement ritual were to be taken outside the camp and burned. In Jesus' time it was forbidden to hold an execution within the city walls of the holy city of Jerusalem. Therefore Jesus was crucified at Golgotha, a small hill which was outside the city walls. Thus according to 13:12 Jesus suffered "outside the gate" in accord with the type or pattern laid out in Leviticus 16. His death was the perfect atoning sacrifice. In light of this typology, the author invites the community to "go to him outside the camp" (13:13) and thus share in the shame that Jesus suffered in his crucifixion. Such action will confirm that their true city is the heavenly Jerusalem ("the one that is to come") and that they have "no lasting city" on earth.

What is true worship for these Jewish Christians? It is not to be found in the sacrifices of the old covenant. Rather, according to 13:15-16, Christian worship is preeminently the praise of God and good deeds. Only here does the author "spiritualize" the concept of sacrifice and relate it to acts of public worship ("a sacrifice of praise") and to good works done by Christians ("God is pleased by sacrifices of that kind," 13:16). Elsewhere, the focus has been on the material sacrifices of the old covenant and the death of Christ interpreted as the perfect sacrifice of the new covenant. The extent to which the "sacrifice of praise" might refer to the Eucharist remains uncertain.

The section ends in 13:17 by returning to the topic of "leaders." Here the leaders are clearly those who presently exercise oversight in the Christian community addressed in this work. The author urges respect for and cooperation with these leaders as being most beneficial for both the leaders and the community.

13:18-25 Final prayers and greetings

The author first in 13:18-19 requests prayers on his own behalf. He attests to the purity of his own intentions ("we have a clear conscience") and hopes to meet soon with the community in person. He clearly knows these people personally, and may well count himself among their leaders (see 13:17).

Then in 13:20-21 the author formulates a prayer on behalf of the community. He prays first (13:20-21a) that God may enable them to

18Pray for us, for we are confident that we have
a clear conscience, wishing to act rightly in every
respect. 19I especially ask for your prayers that I
may be restored to you very soon.
20May the God of peace, who brought up from
the dead the great shepherd of the sheep by the
blood of the eternal covenant, Jesus our Lord,
21furnish you with all that is good, that you may
do his will. May he carry out in you what is pleasing to him through Jesus Christ, to whom be glory
forever [and ever]. Amen.
22Brothers, I ask you to bear with this message
of encouragement, for I have written to you rather
briefly. 23I must let you know that our brother
Timothy has been set free. If he comes soon, I shall
see you together with him. 24Greetings to all your
leaders and to all the holy ones. Those from Italy
send you greetings. 25Grace be with all of you.

do God's will, and then (13:21b) he asks that God may carry out in them what is pleasing to God. God is the beginning and the end of all their good works. The description of Jesus as "the great shepherd of the sheep" is unique in Hebrews (but see John 10:11 and 1 Pet 5:4), whereas the reference to Jesus' resurrection and to "the blood of the eternal covenant" are prominent themes throughout the work.

The request for a favorable reception in 13:22 consists of what is generally regarded as the author's own description of his sermon in written form ("this message of encouragement") and a somewhat disingenuous comment about his having written "rather briefly." The personal information in 13:23 provides a reference to Timothy that is the work's only real link to Paul. Assuming that this is Paul's co-worker, we may suppose that the author knew Timothy. Or perhaps the reference to Timothy was interpolated later to make a connection with Paul and his circle.

The greeting in 13:24a is directed to both the "leaders" (see 13:7, 17) and "all the holy ones" (a common way of referring to Christians). Many scholars find in 13:24b ("those from Italy send you greetings") grounds for supposing that the recipients are in Italy (most likely in Rome), and that the author is conveying greetings from Italians who are living where he is (outside Italy). The text, however, is ambiguous, and it could be read in the opposite way to indicate that the sermon in written form was sent from Italy to another place outside Italy.

The final blessing in 13:25 ("grace be with all of you") is both formulaic (see Titus 3:15) and at the same time expressive of the author's theology of Christ's priestly sacrifice as the ultimate and effective manifestation of God's favor toward humankind.

EXPLORING LESSON SIX

1. Amidst all the distractions of daily life, how are you able to keep your "eyes fixed on Jesus" (12:1-2)? What do you envision yourself "running" or "racing" toward?

2. a) What aspect of suffering is emphasized in Hebrews 12:5-11?

   b) Do you find this view of suffering helpful? Why or why not?

3. Compare and contrast the "old worship" symbolized by Mount Sinai (12:18-21; Exod 19) with the "new worship" symbolized by Mount Zion (12:22-24; see also Rev 21–22).

4. In what way does Jesus' blood speak "more eloquently than that of Abel" (12:24)?

5. How do you envision or understand God as "a consuming fire" (12:29)?

6. a) How is sacrifice described in Hebrews 13:15-16?

   b) How does this view of sacrifice differ from that emphasized elsewhere in Hebrews?

7. a) Who are the "leaders" Christians are called upon to obey in Hebrews 13:17?

b) It may be difficult for us to reconcile Hebrews' call to "obey. . . and defer," given our contemporary emphasis on personal freedom and autonomy. How do you understand this verse in the context of our church today?

8. The last chapter of Hebrews includes a good deal of wisdom and advice on a range of topics. Which verse or instruction from Hebrews 13 do you find most meaningful or helpful?

9. How has your study of Hebrews enriched your understanding of Jesus and his saving work?

CLOSING PRAYER

Prayer

Do not neglect hospitality, for through it some have unknowingly entertained angels. (Heb 13:2)

Jesus, our Lord and Savior, all that we possess is your gracious gift. Grant us the wisdom to see that what you have given us is meant not only to meet our own needs but to provide for the needs of others. Help us always to act with a spirit of generosity and compassion for all. We pray today especially for . . .

PRAYING WITH YOUR GROUP

Because we know that the Bible allows us to hear God's voice, prayer provides the context for our study and sharing. By speaking and listening to God and each other, the discussion often grows to more deeply bond us to one another and to God.

At *the beginning and end of each lesson* simple prayers are provided for individual use, and also may be used within the group setting. Most of the closing prayers provided with each lesson relate directly to a theme from that lesson and encourage you to pray together for people and events in your local community.

Of course, there are many ways to center ourselves in God's presence as we gather together in groups around the word of God. We provide some additional suggestions here knowing you and your group will make prayer a priority as part of your gathering. These are simply alternative ways to pray if your group would like to try something different from those prayers provided in the previous pages.

Conversational Prayer

This form of prayer allows for the group members to pray in their own words in a way that is not intimidating. The group leader begins with Step One, inviting all to focus on the presence of Christ among them. After a few moments of quiet, the group leader invites anyone in the group to voice a prayer or two of thanksgiving; once that is complete, then anyone who has personal intentions may pray in their own words for their needs; finally, the group prays for the needs of others.

A suggested process:
In your own words, speak simple and short prayers to allow time for others to add their voices.

Focus on one "step" at a time, not worrying about praying for everything in your mental list at once.

Step One	Visualize Christ. Welcome him. Imagine him present with you in your group. Allow time for some silence.
Step Two	Gratitude opens our hearts. Use simple words such as, "Thank you, Lord, for . . ."
Step Three	Pray for your own needs knowing that others will pray with you. Be specific and honest. Use "I" and "me" language.

Step Four	Pray for others by name, with love. You may voice your agreement ("Yes, Lord"). End with gratitude for sharing concerns.

Praying Like Ignatius

St. Ignatius Loyola, whose life and ministry are the foundation of the Jesuit community, invites us to enter into Scripture texts in order to experience the scenes, especially scenes of the gospels or other narrative parts of Scripture. Simply put, this is a method of creatively imagining the scene, viewing it from the inside, and asking God to meet you there. Most often, this is a personal form of prayer, but in a group setting, some of its elements can be helpful if you allow time for this process.

A suggested process:

- Select a scene from the chapters in the particular lesson.
- Read that scene out loud in the group, followed by some quiet time.
- Ask group members to place themselves in the scene (as a character, or as an onlooker) so that they can imagine the emotions, responses, and thinking that may have taken place. Notice the details and the tone, and imagine the interaction with the Lord that is taking place.
- Share with the group any insights that came to you in this quiet imagining.
- Allow each person in the group to thank God for some insight and to pray about some request that may have surfaced.

Sacred Reading (or Lectio Divina)

This method of prayer invites us to "listen with the ear of the heart" as St. Benedict's rule would say. We listen to the words and the phrasing, asking God to speak to our innermost being. Again, this method of prayer is most often used in an individual setting but may also be used in an adapted way within a group.

A suggested process:

- Select a scene from the chapters in the particular lesson.
- Read the scene out loud in the group, perhaps two times.
- Ask group members to ponder a word or phrase that stands out to them.
- The group members could then simply speak the word or phrase as a kind of litany of what was meaningful for your group.
- Allow time for more silence to ponder the words that were heard, asking God to reveal to you what message you are meant to hear, how God is speaking to you.
- Follow up with spoken intentions at the close of this group time.

REFLECTING ON SCRIPTURE

Reading Scripture is an opportunity not simply to learn new information but to listen to God who loves you. Pray that the same Holy Spirit who guided the formation of Scripture will inspire you to correctly understand what you read, and empower you to make what you read a part of your life.

The inspired word of God contains layers of meaning. As you make your way through passages of Scripture, whether studying a book of the Bible or focusing on a biblical theme, you may find it helpful to ask yourself these four questions:

> *What does the Scripture passage say?*
> Read the passage slowly and reflectively. Become familiar with it. If the passage you are reading is a narrative, carefully observe the characters and the plot. Use your imagination to picture the scene or enter into it.
>
> *What does the Scripture passage mean?*
> Read the footnotes in your Bible and the commentary provided to help you understand what the sacred writers intended and what God wants to communicate by means of their words.
>
> *What does the Scripture passage mean to me?*
> Meditate on the passage. God's word is living and powerful. What is God saying to you? How does the Scripture passage apply to your life today?
>
> *What am I going to do about it?*
> Try to discover how God may be challenging you in this passage. An encounter with God contains a challenge to know God's will and follow it more closely in daily life. Ask the Holy Spirit to inspire not only your mind but your life with this living word.